PRAISE FOR *Falling for Eli:*

"*Falling for Eli* is a deeply touching memoir, a refreshing and lyrical homage to love and new definitions of motherhood. Shulins is a smart, funny guide on this voyage of discovery and rediscovery, and her 1,200-pound 'baby' Eli will steal your heart."

—Scott Kraft, Senior Editor, *Los Angeles Times*

"Love comes in all sizes and shapes, and Nancy Shulins opens our hearts to endless possibilities with her endearing, beautifully woven story of life with Eli. This book is sure to become a classic, and we'll always want to know what Eli will do next."

—Dolores Barclay, author, and Arts Editor, *The Associated Press*

FALLING *for* ELI

FALLING *for* ELI

How I Lost Heart, Then Gained Hope
Through the Love of a Singular Horse

NANCY SHULINS

Da Capo
∞
LIFE
LONG

A Member of the Perseus Books Group

Design and production by Pauline Brown
Typeset in 13 point Spectrum MT by the Perseus Books Group

Library of Congress Cataloging-in-Publication Data

Shulins, Nancy.
  Falling for Eli : how I lost heart, then gained hope through the love of a singular horse / Nancy Shulins.
      p. cm.
  ISBN 978-0-7382-1527-3 (pbk. : alk. paper) — ISBN 978-0-7382-1581-5 (e-book)
  1. Shulins, Nancy. 2. Human-animal communication.
  3. Horses. I. Title.
  QL785.27.S58 2012
  599.665'5—dc23
                                    2011049131

Published by Da Capo Press
A Member of the Perseus Books Group
www.dacapopress.com

Da Capo Press books are available at special discounts for bulk purchases in the U.S. by corporations, institutions, and other organizations. For more information, please contact the Special Markets Department at the Perseus Books Group, 2300 Chestnut Street, Suite 200, Philadelphia, PA, 19103, or call (800) 810-4145, ext. 5000, or e-mail special.markets@perseusbooks.com.

For Christee: gifted trainer,
patient teacher, loyal friend.
If not for you, this equestrian would
undoubtedly be a pedestrian.

AUTHOR'S NOTE

THIS IS A TRUE STORY. I have depicted the events, conversations, and people involved based on my best recollections of them, though I have changed some of the names and identifying details to protect privacy. Although conflict is part of the story, as it is part of life, the perspective that comes with the passing of time has led me to the realization that everyone in these pages has given me something of value. All have been my teachers, and for that, I am thankful.

PROLOGUE

AUTUMN 1996

I CAN STILL PICTURE THE CARROT CAKE, a rich triple-decker affair studded with raisins and crowned with glossy clouds of whipped cream. I close my eyes and I'm back in my neighbor's living room up the block on a spectacular Indian summer afternoon, surrounded by girlfriends in blazers and boots. "Business casual," someone had said, still a fresh concept back then.

Before me, a pile of presents teeters precariously. As I work my way through them, my friend Alex snatches each bow and sticks it to a paper plate I'm made to wear on my head "for good luck."

Gift-wise, they're all here, all the classics: The colorful plastic pail filled with bath towels and sponges; the stylish tote bag stocked with wipes, swabs, and creams. There are soft, fleecy things, padded things, clever things with Velcro straps, things I have lusted after for a very long time.

One minute I'm laughing, the next I'm in tears, over everything from the cake to the gifts, thanking my friends repeatedly for having done this for me, for understanding how much this ritual means.

We're all a bit looped—champagne in broad daylight will do that—and though I'm happy to wear the ridiculous ribbon hat, I draw the line at letting them measure my stomach.

This isn't the party I pictured all the years I secretly dreamed of this day, little fantasies that helped me endure every painful procedure that got me to where I am now. Someday, I'd tell myself, while being biopsied, inseminated, or injected with dye, this part will be over, and my friends and I will celebrate over mini-cupcakes in a room filled with spray roses and alphabet blocks.

This late in the game, though, only the friends are the same. They're the women who held their breath and my hand while I struggled to achieve what had come so effortlessly for them: Katie, with her four children; Nancy with three; Claire and Alex, with two apiece; Amy with one.

Their babies grew to be babysitters while I ran my obstacle course again and again, racing from injection to injection, ultrasound to ultrasound, miscarriage to miscarriage, until now.

I savor each bite and linger over each gift, but as November afternoons tend to do, this one comes to an end much too soon. I blot my eyes with a Winnie the Pooh napkin and propose a final toast: To new life and old friends.

Then I walk home with my treasures, asking myself: *Is this real?*

And the answer comes back: *Yes and no.*

Like the pictures that change when you tilt the card they've been printed on, I have only to shift my viewing angle ever so slightly for the diaper pail to morph into a feed bucket, the changing pad into a saddle pad.

And with that, my baby shower reverts to a "bridle" shower.

Because it isn't a boy *or* a girl. It's a gelding.

My very own 1,254-pound bundle of joy.

one

SPRING 1995

ETTING GO OF A DREAM IS A PROCESS, a series of openings and closings of the hand, as you watch the magic dust you've been cradling so carefully trickle away in thin streams. It's a progression, one that cannot be rushed. The key is to practice losing a bit at a time, lest you fall apart when you see it's all gone.

I spilled the first of my dust in my doctor's office on a sunny spring morning in 1995, after yet another ultrasound failed to locate a heartbeat where just a week earlier there had been two.

I let loose another trickle a couple of months later, after an obligatory meeting with the head of the egg-donor program at Yale. My doctor wanted me to hear all the options and so, like a dutiful daughter, I went. But my husband and I were already in debt after years of infertility treatments, and the cost of a donor egg, plus in vitro fertilization, was well beyond our reach.

Even if we could have afforded it, I felt too gun-shy to undergo yet another procedure with no guarantee of results. If my goal was a baby—*any* baby—didn't it make more sense to start with one already born? A friend's sister had recently adopted a beautiful Chinese baby girl. Neither the cost nor the red tape involved had discouraged me from elaborate fantasies of following suit.

My husband, however, was another story. My wonderful husband, who'd been ambivalent about kids from the start, had made it clear all along that adoption was a bridge too far. I couldn't fault him. As it was, Mark had been unfailingly supportive and sympathetic, administering my nightly shots, producing semen even before his morning coffee, and comforting me over each failed attempt.

The sad truth is that we'd come a little late to the baby business. I was thirty-six; Mark, a year older. For the first four years of our marriage, we'd focused on our careers and each other. I never expected my priorities to shift as abruptly and drastically as they did, in a manner that was less rational decision than biological imperative.

Living in Fairfield County, Connecticut, was like living in a fertility theme park. I was surrounded by pregnant women and women with babies. Watching Mark with his three brothers' children only inflamed my ever-increasing baby lust. As an uncle, he was a natural—gentle, playful, and inventive. Anyone could see how great a father he would be.

But by the time I was ready to consider adopting other people's babies, the bulk of our married agenda had been dictated by our struggle to reproduce. "There has to be more to life than that," Mark said.

Although I was far from convinced, it was clearly time to find out. To be fair, the plus side of my ledger was not exactly empty. In addition to my marriage, I had a demanding and fulfilling job writing national features for the Associated Press in New York City, where Mark worked as a supervising editor. I had Jake, my beautiful Labrador retriever. Born the very day of my first miscarriage, he'd been my constant companion and gentle web-footed nurse ever since.

I had my older sister, Debbie, and her kids, five-year-old Zoe and nine-year-old Ben, my wonderful substitute children, their young lives unfolding just two streets away, enabling me to be their first babysitter. Our house was the first place they'd ever walked to alone, holding hands as they made their way up the sidewalk.

That was the plus side. On the downside, we were living in the suburban capital of kids and that was unlikely to change. If we wanted the house and the trees and the dog, I was going to have to find a way to cope.

A nice, long vacation seemed a good start. We settled on the Pacific Northwest and flew to Seattle for a meandering ten-day drive along the coast.

It was spring, the season of fresh starts, though all around me things seemed to be dying, particularly the salmon at the Issaquah Salmon Hatchery, where we'd set off on the self-guided tour. There, mesmerized by the sight of the salmon flinging themselves at the fish ladder, driven by instinct to spawn and die, I finally opened my hand and let the rest of my magic dust go. *It's not worth it,* I thought. *Any fool can see that.*

I remember laughing a lot on the rest of that trip, having lightened up at long last. We drove from Seattle to Portland, visiting friends (and their children) along the way. Being together, just the two of us, felt good. *I can do this,* I thought. But what had been a no-brainer on the Left Coast ceased to be obvious back on the right, where the squeaky parade of baby strollers, Big Wheels, and scooters converged daily smack in the middle of Hickory Lane, directly in front of my house.

Within days, I'd regressed. Despite the return of nice weather, I stopped taking Jake to the park rather than risking an encounter with my neighbors, the Fertile Myrtles. Their latest crop of infants had arrived right on schedule, one a month, every month, as reliable as the Fruit-of-the-Month Club. Had I managed to stay pregnant I'd be out there now, too, wheeling a stroller in the sunshine and bitching about sleep deprivation.

Instead, I was hiding in my house, overdosing on sleep. Although I was supposed to be working from home, I couldn't write. Nor could I cook or clean, read a book, hit the gym, or shop for groceries. Seeing friends or running errands was out of the question. I was fixated on the hole at the center of my life, the empty space where the kids should have been. It loomed so much larger than anything I could imagine trying to fill it with that I would spend entire days doing little else but grappling with its unwieldy dimensions.

And so I was at a loss the afternoon Mark called from work to tell me he'd been chatting with a colleague who had horses. Would I like to visit her barn and meet them?

Horses. The word rang a faint, distant bell, like an echo from a previous life.

I could still picture the trio of horses I'd known: Rhythm, the ancient white lesson horse of my New Hampshire childhood; Hamlet, the rangy chestnut I took on trail rides when I was a small-town reporter in my twenties; and Erin, the bay mare who was at my disposal the summer I taught at the University of Vermont.

Since then, aside from my reproductive campaign, I'd focused on my marriage and my career. I'd been lucky at both love and work. Horses, though, had fallen by the wayside despite my lifelong passion for them, too expensive, time-consuming, and impractical for a pair of commuters with a bloated mortgage and a postage-stamp lawn.

Back in the here and now I felt a pang at the mention of them, some plucked string that still vibrated after all these years. I willed it to stop. I was too big a mess to meet anyone. I was fashioning some sort of gracious excuse when Mark simply handed a woman named Susan his phone.

The better part of an hour later, I was printing out directions to a boarding barn twenty miles away. Without meaning to, I'd accepted Susan's invitation to come for a visit the following Sunday—and what's more, I was no longer sad.

With that on my calendar to look forward to, for the first time in weeks I felt something besides grief, something buoyant and viable that enabled me to grab my keys, hop in my car, and wave to the moms as I drove off with Jake. I hadn't a clue where we were going, but we were goddamn well *going.* We were leaving the house. It was a start.

two

JUNE 1995

O N THE SUNDAY I AM TO MEET SUSAN, I wake up much too early and dress in the closest facsimile of a riding out-fit I've been able to pull together on short notice: a pair of beige pull-on tights with suede patches at the knees made to look (sort of) like britches, and a dusty pair of lace-ups vaguely reminiscent of the paddock boots of yesteryear. I'm aiming for a look—like something out of a classic Ralph Lauren ad—and missing it by a mile. I look like I'm bound for a rodeo clown convention.

A short while later, when Mark and Jake return home from their hike and take in my cheesy ensemble, my cheeks redden. "I know I look ridiculous, but she told me to wear riding clothes," I say, "and I don't really have any."

"Does that mean you'll get to ride?"

I shrug. "Good question. I have no idea."

"Well, be careful. And have fun."

I kiss his cheek, scrounge some carrots from the vegetable bin, and head out.

With plenty of time to kill, I opt for the back roads. As I drive through the woodsy Connecticut countryside, I admire the myriad shades of green, reminders of my Northern New England youth. Tomboy that I was, I preferred outside to in, and spent hours in the woods with its lush carpet of mosses, pine needles, wildflowers, and ferns.

I knew the location of every lady's slipper within a half-mile radius of my house. I made bouquets out of starflowers, ink out of sumac, and stationery from the papery skin of fallen birches. A secret cave carved into a hillside a block away from my house sheltered me from the sudden storms that are a hallmark of the North Country's fleeting summers.

Passing a small backyard barn a few miles from my house, I slow down to look for its occupant, an American Paint Horse. I'm rewarded with a glimpse of her grazing in her paddock alongside her foal, a tiny, perfect echo of her. The sighting, always a highlight when I travel this road, seems almost magical today. As I pass them, my husband's question reverberates in my head: *Does that mean you'll get to ride?* At the prospect, I feel that old familiar blend of giddy excitement and stomach-churning nerves. I was never a very confident rider. I'm not built for it; much like the rest of me, my legs are too short.

Besides, the best riders I know learned as children, just like the best swimmers, downhill skiers, and tennis players. I wasn't raised to break a sweat and keep on playing. I was raised to sit in the shade and sip lemonade till it passed. I come from a long line of non-athletes. The Shulinses are perspiration-averse.

We're not great swimmers, either. Even though our summer cottage on Lake Sunapee had its own private beach, I wasn't allowed to go in over my head. Downhill skiing—the ubiquitous New Hampshire pastime—was too dangerous. My father lost an eye in a childhood skiing accident. To protect against a similar fate, I wasn't allowed to start learning how to ski till I was ten—practically a granny by local standards.

I have no recollection of my first skiing lesson. But I have total recall of my first pony ride five years earlier at a grade school carnival. I remember hurrying past the popcorn balls and the fishing pole games as if pulled by some magnetic force to the ponies that stood in a clump in the shade, swishing their tails at the flies.

It cost two quarters for two trips around the ball field, led by a boy who smelled like a pony himself. I had $2 saved. The boy picked me up and set me down in a worn leather saddle on a pony that was white with brown flecks.

I fell in love with that docile old pony and the thrill of sitting high above the ground as we circled the small, sun-splashed field again and again, at a pace so glacial I barely made it home in time for supper.

I come to a stop sign and realize I stopped paying attention to Susan's directions some time ago. Where am I? I have no idea. I drive straight through the intersection and continue on till I come to the church that means I've overshot my destination. I pull into the parking lot, turn around and head back the way I came.

I've gone less than a mile when I see Oakwood Farm just ahead on the left, a traditional red barn perched on a rise and a newer-looking weathered one below it. There's an outdoor riding ring surrounded by neatly fenced paddocks.

I pull into the driveway and see five horses running the fence line in a large grassy pasture off to one side, nipping each other's flanks, tossing their heads, and trotting off with their tails carried high. I breathe in their scent and drink in the sight of them.

I am in Xanadu.

I am in Oz.

As instructed, I park alongside the horse trailers across from the pristine Georgian colonial that overlooks the property. Admiring the English cutting garden surrounding the pool, I walk down the steep dirt driveway that leads to the lower barn.

The big sliding doors are wide open, revealing a cavernous indoor riding arena, deserted on this beautiful day. Just past the indoor ring, I see a second opening, a long, narrow aisle lined with box stalls. Like Dorothy in reverse, I step out of the Technicolor sunshine and into the dim, russet barn.

For the moment it takes for my eyes to adjust, I inhale the heady aroma of horses, manure, wood shavings, and hay, with top notes of worn saddle leather, and realize how much I have missed it. I then head down the corridor, treading carefully along the buckled concrete floor, peering into stalls as I go, hoping for a glimpse of an actual horse—maybe even a nuzzle—but nobody's home.

At the far end, I encounter a woman who looks to be well into her sixties grooming a Welsh pony whose white hair and dour expression match hers to a T. The brass nameplate on the open stall door identifies the pony as White Lightning and his owner as Edith.

"Hi there," I say, smiling brightly.

She glares at me and says nothing.

"I'm meeting Susan. Do you know if she's here?"

Silence. Could she be hard of hearing?

I ramp up the volume. *"I'm supposed to meet Susan here."*

"Heard you the first time," she mutters. "They're all Susans. Which one?"

I reach for the note in my pocket to double-check, as if I hadn't committed it to memory, as if I hadn't read and reread it all week. "Strong."

"Not here," she says, and goes back to her grooming.

What to do? I glance at my watch. I'm still early. Straight ahead, just outside the barn in the outdoor riding ring, I see a striking young woman with auburn hair whose very long legs are wrapped around an enormous bay gelding. Intent on their work, neither notices me, and I hang back a bit so that they won't.

There's some kind of seamless connection between them, as if their bodies and minds are one and the same. How else to account for the lightness of the big horse's movements, the supple ease with which he transitions from gait to gait? One minute he's practically trotting in place; the next, his legs are so extended he appears to be flying as he trots across the ring on a diagonal line. Now he's moving forward and sideways at the same time (!), his outside legs crossing over the inside ones with each stride; and all this with no discernible signals from the rider.

I hold my breath as I watch them defy gravity again and again. Whatever it is, this magical human-horse pas de deux, I want to learn how to do it.

Too soon, the woman brings the horse to a halt and lengthens the reins, enabling him to stretch. She pats his muscular neck and notices me standing there awestruck. "Can I help you with something?"

I tell her I'm waiting for Susan Strong. "But I'm in no hurry. That was so amazing to watch. What was it? That you were doing, I mean. Are you going to do some more? And what kind of horse is he? Is he yours?"

She smiles down at me. The horse is even bigger up close. "No, he's not mine. I'm his trainer. He's Hanoverian and we were doing dressage. Do you ride?"

"Yes. I mean, no! God, not in years. And never anything even remotely like that."

She smiles again. "Well, I'd better cool him down." They amble off toward the pasture beyond the ring. Only then do I see the sweat, as thick as shaving cream between his hind legs, an indication of how hard he just worked, however effortless it appeared.

I'm still watching them when a slender, attractive woman with cropped dark hair and legs almost as long as the redhead's comes up alongside me on a beefy chestnut glossy with sweat. "You must be Nancy. I'm Susan."

I nod. "Good to meet you. And who's this handsome guy?" I pat his neck the way the redhead patted the bay.

"This is Frank. Feel like helping me clean him up?"

The grin that lights my face could best be measured in megawatts. Susan smiles back. "I'll take that as a yes."

* * *

WITH FRANK IN THE WASH STALL, secured by a pair of wall-mounted nylon cross ties clipped to his halter, Susan instructs me on the art of the bath. I man the hose, wetting him down, first with room-temperature water, beginning with his legs and gradually working my way up. With horses, she says, it's always best to avoid abrupt changes, not only in temperature, but in diet, exercise, and routine. Their bulk belies the delicacy of their systems, which are complex and easily overwhelmed.

Somehow, I'd never managed to learn even this much in the time I had spent around horses. Eager to soak up this new knowledge, I ask endless questions and apologize for knowing so little, but Susan waves it off.

"Nah," she says. "You don't learn this stuff from riding the occasional lesson horse."

As I lather Frank with a sea sponge dunked in a bucket of sudsy water, Susan gives me the lay of the land. The striking red-haired woman is Jackie and this is her barn. She leases it from the owner of the Colonial house and rents out the stalls, most of them to her own students. She's an excellent trainer and a highly accomplished rider, and she runs the place with an iron fist. She keeps her own horses here; if I was impressed watching her on the bay, wait till I see her ride her own new Danish warmblood.

Which reminds me: "What exactly is dressage?" I ask Susan. "I know about Western and English, but dressage is new to me."

"It's a bit complicated," Susan says, "but dressage is basically a type of training that strengthens and improves a horse's movements. It's done on the flat, and it's the deepest seat you can have on a horse. Some people think of it as a kind of horse ballet that teaches the rider to sit tall and communicate using subtle aids. It teaches the horse to be more responsive and to carry more of its weight on its hind legs."

"Ah," I reply. The deepest seat? Horse ballet? I have no idea what she's talking about.

With tousled hair and flushed faces, the other boarders begin trickling back from the day's adventures. From what

I can see as they pass us en route to the tack room, I'm surrounded by women all more or less my age, and—Hallelujah!—not one of them is pushing a stroller.

I'm about to ask Susan for a breakdown of the barn's demographics when a strawberry blonde with a faceful of freckles sticks her head in. "Are you going to be much longer?"

"We're almost done," Susan says. "Bonnie, meet Nancy."

I extend a soapy hand and she gives it a businesslike shake before returning to her horse, a young-looking Paint.

Next, I meet Marti, a ninety-eight-pound bundle of energy with Betty Boop features and a talented chestnut gelding that's considered a minor star at this barn, and Missy, an athletic market researcher with a ready smile and no horse of her own, though she half-leases somebody else's.

"Really? You can lease a horse?" It sounds odd to me, but Susan assures me it's done all the time. "Depending on the deal you make, you might pay half the board bill and get to ride three or four days a week."

I nod my head and try to look thoughtful as my heart does a little dance in my chest; part-time horse ownership, here I come! Before I can get too giddy, though, Frank paws the floor and reclaims my attention with his high forehead and worried expression, his long, powerful body and short, muscular legs.

I learn that he is half Quarter Horse and half Thoroughbred, a breed unto itself known as the Appendix Quarter Horse. It's a good pairing, combining the power and incomparable short-distance speed of the heavily muscled Quarter Horse with the leaner, more refined Thoroughbred. The result is a horse with the size and endurance to excel not only at racing, but also at ranch work, jumping, trail riding, and more.

I rinse Frank and gently scrape off the excess water with a squeegee, half wishing I could wash him all over again for the pure pleasure of touching his skin, as silken and soft as a baby's. With Susan beside me, I lead him outside to eat grass and air dry before returning him to his stall for his supper. Although it's getting to be suppertime for humans as well, I'm reluctant to tear myself away from this place, reluctant to see such a perfect day end.

The following weekend, Susan invites me back to Oakwood to watch her work Frank. Determined to be the best observer she's ever seen, I'm perched on a bench in the "indoor," as everyone calls it, focused only on them when someone yells, *"Door!"* and I jump. I look over and there's Missy laughing at me. Red faced, I laugh too, and she comes over to join me, explaining the etiquette of calling out before entering the indoor so as not to spook the horses.

"That makes perfect sense," I say, "and I can't believe I didn't know that."

"Why would you? You've probably never ridden at a barn with an indoor."

I think a minute. "You're right, I haven't. But that's just the tip of the iceberg of what I don't know."

"Well, you've come to the right place."

So it seems. After Susan finishes with Frank—and I finish treating him to two enormous bunches of carrots— I return to watch Missy ride her half-leased horse. More handsome than pretty, with chin-length brown hair and a strong yet compact body, she cuts an elegant figure in the saddle. I admire her quiet hands, secure seat, and unfailing composure, even when her horse lets out an exuberant buck in celebration of the sheer joy of movement.

Fun as it is watching the other women ride, I find myself aching to join them. Every sight—every sound—reawakens some long-submerged memory of how riding feels. I have all I can do to keep from rolling my hips in concert with Missy's as she canters by. I hardly notice that Susan has returned to sit beside me until she asks if I'd be interested in taking some lessons on Frank.

"Was it that obvious?" I ask. She nods, laughing, and I give her a one-armed hug.

* * *

TWO DAYS LATER, I'm just the tiniest bit nervous (read: quivering wreck) as I prepare for my first lesson with Jackie. I manage to curry and brush Frank, pick his hooves clean, and get him saddled, bridled, booted, and ready to rumble in just under an hour, only four times longer than Susan's estimate. I'm rather pleased.

I cross tacking him up off my list of worries and move on to the next: that he will take advantage of my obvious inexperience and plant me headfirst in the nearest pile of manure. I lead him into the empty indoor—making sure to yell "Door!"—and, per Susan's instructions, hand-walk him once around before tightening his girth.

Then Jackie comes in and holds him for me as I ascend the mounting block, place my left foot in the stirrup, and swing my right leg over his back. That much I remember how to do. But my legs are so much shorter than Susan's we'll need to make new, higher holes for the stirrups. Jackie goes off to fetch her hole punch, leaving Frank and me unattended.

"Any last-minute advice for me?" I'd asked Susan over the phone.

"Just try to remember to breathe."

I take a deep breath, then another, trying to recall my last ride. It's been years. Decades, even. Whatever happened to muscle memory? Mine doesn't seem to be working. "It's like riding a bike," Susan had said. I think, *No, it's not! It's like riding a horse.*

Frank lets out a sigh that I take to mean he's unhappy. He then starts pawing the ground, confirming it. *Where the hell is Jackie? What's taking her so long?* I consider dismounting until she returns, but I hate to be that big a weenie, at least not in the first five minutes.

So I give Frank a cluck and we set off at a meandering walk and nothing terrible happens, despite my dangling stirrups and lack of supervision. The vulnerability I felt when I first climbed aboard with nothing in front of me— *No seatbelt! No airbag! No OnStar!*—begins ever-so-slightly to fade. We're on our second lap by the time Jackie returns with the tool to find us at the far end of the ring, me grinning, Frank ambling, things more or less under control.

*　＊＊

MY FIRST FEW LESSONS leave me achy and elated, even as they strip me of any modest delusions I may have had about my competence as a rider. It turns out I know next to nothing. The first thing I learn is that there's a world of difference between piloting a horse and simply going along for the ride.

Given how little I've done of the former, Jackie wants to start with the basics. Fine by me.

My first challenge is to put Frank where I want him, not only in terms of the ring's geography, but also the various regions of his body: his haunches, his shoulders, his neck. If I'm to accomplish all that, I'll need to shorten my reins to maintain a soft but steady connection with his mouth. But I can't very well shorten the reins without somehow shortening the horse; to do *that*, I need to pull him together. To pull him together, I need to use more leg. That I don't *have* any more leg is a moot point. So ends my introduction to Dressage 101. I am at once thrilled and baffled.

I'm also thankful that the edge that often creeps into Jackie's tone when she's training her more seasoned students is nowhere in evidence when she's training me. If anything, she's more patient with me than I am with myself, though Missy warns me not to get too used to it. "Just remember, you're still on your honeymoon," she says, after having emerged soaked with sweat from her own session, looking as though Jackie had turned the hose on her.

After my semiweekly lessons, I linger awhile to chat with whoever's around, eager to relinquish my newcomer status and begin to feel a bit more at home. I introduce myself to the boarders, admire their horses, and memorize both sets of names, much as I've done with the moms on Hickory Lane. Like them, the boarders apologize profusely for the slobber their darlings spatter all over my shirt, apologies that bother me more than the spots for implying I belong less to the group that cares about horses than I do the one that cares about stains.

Short of wearing a sign to the contrary, I don't know what more I can do. I'm so tired of pressing my nose to the glass, tired of looking in from the outside. *Maybe I'm through trying. Maybe I'm done.* The thought hits me as I'm on my way home. Why let other people dictate where they think I belong? Why not just decide for myself?

Something inside me is beginning to break free, something seismic and deep that for lack of a better name, I decide to call happiness. Driving home in a rosy glow of sweat, grime, and horse drool, I realize I'm happier than I've been in years.

I am *so* happy, in fact, that when my sister and her husband unveil an elaborate plan to move to Los Angeles at the end of the summer to pursue their dream of becoming screenwriters, I dismiss it completely. *This will pass,* I tell myself as my nephew bangs away on my piano after school. *This will pass SOON,* I repeat on the weekend, as I hoist my niece onto the counter to stir chocolate chips into cookie dough with one of my long wooden spoons.

My denial continues unabated right into the summer, even as my brother-in-law paints the outside of their house, hauls asbestos out of their basement, and installs a new gas water heater. *Just a whim. Not to worry.*

At the barn one Friday night, with our imperial six-foot-tall trainer away on vacation, Missy, Bonnie, Susan, and I linger past the official 9:00 PM lights-out for some additional girl-bonding in the tack room. Our discussion drifts back and forth between Missy's ongoing search for a horse of her own and the empty stall left by the recent, abrupt departure of a boarder who didn't do things Jackie's way.

I don't recall who does the first Jackie impression, only that each of us has one. All gently poke fun at her controlling tendencies; all are funny without being mean.

"Wouldn't it be great to sneak in a horse and pretend Missy's bought it?" Susan says to hoots of laughter.

"Without Jackie's approval? Yeah, that'd be fun all right," Bonnie adds, "especially if it were a swaybacked old plug."

"Hey, I know," I say. "Let's borrow a cow from the farm down the road. We could put a halter and polo wraps on it."

We're all in hysterics imagining Jackie's reaction to the sight of a cow in her proper dressage barn. I'm still chuckling over this the next morning, when I stop by my sister's to pick up Bessie, her German wirehaired pointer, for a romp at the park with my Jake.

"Where is everybody?"

"They all went for a bike ride," Debbie says. "Maybe I'll go with you. I feel like I never see you anymore."

"Great!"

And it is, until I'm dropping her off at her house afterward and she begins one too many sentences with, "Once we're in L.A. . . ."

"Okay, enough already," I say in my most condescending tone. "Let's face facts. You are *not* moving to Los Angeles."

"Yes, actually we *are*," she says, suddenly furious. She grabs Bessie, gets out of the car, and slams the door hard, leaving me and Jake sitting there to finally face facts.

I return home with eyes brimming. "They're really going," I wail.

Mark hugs me and rubs my back the way he does when I'm upset over something he's powerless to change.

"Maybe the house won't sell," he offers.

But of course it does, practically overnight. Faced with the loss of my substitute children, I find myself gravitating to the barn more and more. Seeing less of my sister and the kids enables me to stage a dress rehearsal for their impending absence, once again spilling that magic dust a trickle at a time.

Over the years, I'd often borrowed Ben and Zoe to take the curse off my childlessness; with one or both of them in tow I could go out in public and do nice, normal, everyday things. I could shop for groceries, walk the dog, or run errands without worrying about what people thought: that I was some sort of child-hater, or—more to the point—a woman too defective to reproduce.

Strange as it sounds now, even to me, at the time that was a major concern. It was hard to go anywhere in Fairfield County without seeing overwhelming numbers of mothers and kids. Without Ben and Zoe as my armor, I imagined people looking at me as if I were some kind of freak. *It's 10:00 AM. Do you know where your children are?*

Apart from that, I couldn't imagine what life would be like with my only sibling a continent away. My older sister—so much like me, yet so emphatically her own person—had always counseled me through life's speed bumps, and vice versa. Our two-and-a-half-year age difference, so impervious during our childhood, ceased to matter once we were in high school. From then on, we'd been each other's best friends, reality checks, and support systems.

As adults, we'd lived within a few blocks of one another for the better part of a decade, first in Hoboken, New Jersey, when we commuted to jobs in the city, then in Connecticut. Along with nearsightedness and naturally curly hair, we shared a dry sense of humor and an innate distrust of authority that had long since made us mouthy partners in crime.

I feel like I never see you anymore.

I know. But I really need the barn right now.

The truth is I need the barn a little too much. I'm using the place like a drug. Unfortunately, reality begins to interfere with my high, as when I discover the trainer whom I've come to idolize turns out to have a frightening temper.

I first see it one Sunday morning as I'm watching Jackie tighten the girth on a boarder's horse. The horse lays his ears back and bites the air, normally a misdemeanor. Not this time. Jackie grabs the nearest object— a toilet plunger—and starts whacking him with it. Although the punishment clearly does not fit the crime, the intensity of her anger scares me to the point where all I can do is watch in stunned silence.

Fortunately, a bystander wrestles the plunger from her hand and tells her to chill. Jackie calms down quickly and considerably, but I still can't erase the disturbing image.

However extreme, Jackie's knee-jerk reaction to bad horse behavior isn't all that unusual. A horse that nips may very well be summarily smacked; a horse that threatens to kick—or that actually *does*—may be on the receiving end of a swift kick himself. Such corrections, handled quickly and judiciously, can put a stop to dangerous behavior, negating the need for further punishment in the future. But if the trainer goes overboard and loses her temper, the horse also loses the opportunity to learn from the mistake. Much as I'd like to think of Jackie's loss of control as an isolated incident, however, I strongly suspect otherwise. Now that I've witnessed her famous temper firsthand, I can only aim to steer clear of it in the future.

Less than a month before the movers are due at my sister's, I'm warming up for a lesson on Frank when I feel him take a bad step, as if onto an unmoored dock. I immediately dismount and feel his legs the way I've seen others do. Because I don't really expect to feel much, I'm alarmed to discover that even to my inexperienced hand, his lower left front leg feels decidedly warmer than the right.

I summon Jackie, who feels the leg and confirms the bad news: Frank has strained a tendon. He may even have torn it. Either way, it'll take three to six months to heal.

"Did I do this to him?"

"Absolutely not," Jackie says. "He probably did it in turnout. So. Do you know what to do?"

I look at her quizzically.

"Go hose his leg. I'll get Jesse to show you."

Great, I say to myself. *Just wonderful.* Jesse, the barn manager and resident cold fish, is the one person with whom I have zero rapport. She prefers not to acknowledge my existence, speaking to me grudgingly if at all. I have no idea why.

My concern over Frank is now nearly eclipsed by my dread at the prospect of Jesse helping me with him.

I lead poor, limping Frank back to the wash stall, where I feed him carrots with one hand and cold-hose his injured leg with the other, talking to him soothingly all the while. Twenty minutes later, when I finally stand up, my foot is asleep, my back aches, and my britches are nearly as wet as Frank's leg. Next time, along with a towel, I'll remember to bring something with me to sit on.

Jesse is waiting for us on the aisle with her nose out of joint and her first-aid supplies neatly aligned: a tub of poultice; a strip of brown paper torn from an empty feed sack; two thick, padded lengths of woven cotton, each roughly the size of a pillowcase; and two rolled bandages the width of my hand, made out of some kind of stretchy fabric.

She's already exuding an air of impatience that won't help and isn't meant to. "Watch what I do." She wets the paper and uses it to scoop out a big blob of poultice, which she smears thickly over the lower part of Frank's injured leg as if she were icing a cake. She covers the wet poultice with the wet paper, the paper with the pillow wrap, and the pillow wrap with the bandage, which she winds around and around the lower leg from top to bottom to hold the wrap in place, neatly securing the end with a built-in Velcro fastener.

"Got it?"

"Poultice-paper-pillow. Got it."

"Here," she says, thrusting the other pillow wrap and bandage at me. "Do the other leg."

"What for?" I ask. "He only hurt the one."

"I know, but we wrap them both."

"Really? Why?"

"Because we *do,*" she says, pointedly checking her watch. "Just dry-wrap it. Hurry up. No poultice or paper."

"Okay." I take the pillow wrap and wind it around his right front leg exactly the way Jesse did, except—"Wrong! You're doing it counterclockwise. On this leg, you need to wrap clockwise. Otherwise you could bow a tendon."

Although I have no idea what that means, this is neither the time nor the person to ask. I start over but screw up my second attempt by failing to hold onto the pillow wrap tightly enough. As I'm reaching for the bandage, it unspools from Frank's leg.

"You have to hold onto it," Jesse says, exasperated.

With gritted teeth, I rewrap, tucking the bandage into the pillow wrap and winding it COUNTERCLOCKWISE around the uninjured leg, only—"You started too high. You're going to run out of bandage before the whole wrap is covered," Jesse says loudly.

I hear a heavy sigh and look up to see a woman I recognize from the upper barn with her horse all tacked up, en route to the indoor. We're blocking the aisle. "Are you about done?" she asks.

"No. Sorry," I mutter. I stand up and undo one of the cross ties, gently moving Frank over to let them pass.

I'm squatting back down for another attempt when Jesse grabs the pillow wrap from my hand. "Never mind. I'll just do it myself," she says. "I don't have time to stand around and play teacher."

Hating her, I slink off to the tack room to gather my belongings and head home, where, last I checked, I still knew how to do things.

I know I shouldn't take it personally, but I do. Jesse's attitude shadows me into the next day, when I find myself delaying my trip to the barn to avoid running into her.

I vacillate between anger and hurt as I fixate on her treatment of me. What had I done to deserve it? Nothing I could think of, other than having come to the horse world a little late. This seems to be a recurring theme in my life. Well, we can't all be so lucky as to grow up in the saddle. Better late than never, I would think.

That evening, I'm grazing Frank in near-total darkness when I make out the familiar shape of Missy's truck pulling in. "Do you think you might have time to show me how to wrap a leg?" I ask as she approaches. "Jesse tried, but—"

"Yeah, I heard."

"*What?*"

"There aren't any secrets here. Think of this place as a big junior high," she says. "Jesse's the bitchy head cheerleader."

I snicker at this and Missy links her arm with mine. "Come on," she says. "Let's go pillow-wrap something. We can pretend it's Jesse's mouth."

* * *

ALTHOUGH I WANT TO HELP care for Frank during his convalescence, I don't want to have to wait till it's over before I can ride again. As it is, it's been over a week. All my soreness is gone and I miss it.

Jackie comes to my rescue, arranging for me to half-lease a horse owned by one of her token male boarders. A cross between a draft horse and a Standardbred, or trotter, Clarabelle reminds me of the proverbial old gray mare, plodding and trustworthy, comfy as an old couch. On Clara I can go anywhere.

We clomp around the neighborhood by ourselves, something I never quite dared do on Frank, roaming the few remaining trails that have yet to sprout the McMansions we all know are coming, and sauntering through the subdivisions that have already come. The tension between what was once mostly farmland and the development that's encroaching on it is a preview of what's coming to well-heeled towns throughout Fairfield County.

Past barking dogs and children's birthday parties, hissing sprinklers and whining weed whackers, my sensible, sturdy girl and I take in the sights as the summer winds down around us.

The only drawback to Clarabelle is that I have to share her. I shared Frank, too, of course, though Susan spoiled me from the start by refusing to take my money even as she made him available more or less whenever I asked.

Under the terms of my new, somewhat more formal arrangement, I'm entitled to ride Clarabelle three days a week. But her owner gets first dibs and he prefers sunny weekends. I get rainy days and weeknights, with that 9:00 PM curfew.

More often than not when it's my turn to ride, I duck out of work to catch the 6:07 PM train at Grand Central, putting me back in Connecticut an hour later. Provided I hurry and the traffic isn't too bad, I can be at the barn by 7:50. I then tear into the tack room, peel off my work clothes, and pull on my britches and boots. I curry, then brush the saddle area of Clara's back to clear away any dirt or debris, throw on her saddle, and have a half hour to ride in an indoor arena clogged with other women doing the same mad dash.

The hidden blessing in all of this racing around is that it leaves me very little time to mope. When my sister and her family finally leave for the coast, I manage to let them go without falling apart. I see them off with hugs and kisses and enough food to last them till Indiana. Then I head straight for the barn.

three

AUTUMN 1995

FRANK REMAINS ON STALL REST into the fall with noth-ing to do but monitor my comings and goings. His worried eyes and hopeful nicker make it impossible for me to sneak by him. Many nights, rather than try, I turn the lights off at 9:00 PM, obeying the letter if not the intent of the law, and creep into his stall to feed him treats and keep him company for a while in the dark.

On weekends, when there's more time, I hand-walk him for twenty minutes, all that he's allowed, as we wait for the tendon to heal.

Although I miss riding him, I love caring for him. I also find it incredibly bonding. We become a herd of two as I take on the various roles of nurse, trainer, stable mate, groom, and masseuse. When Susan suddenly wavers on the eve of a long-awaited trip to Europe, I encourage her to go, promising to look after Frank in her absence.

"You've been looking forward to this for months," I remind her. "I promise Frank will be fine. I'll keep him walked, groomed, and entertained. I won't even let him notice you're gone."

I take a couple days off from work to ride Clarabelle and lavish attention on the shut-in. Jackie teases me about spoiling him, and though I'm hard-pressed to deny it, I do have an ulterior motive. On some level, I'm trying horse ownership on for size, luxuriating in the feeling of responsibility for a life other than mine. Not that I'm solely responsible for Frank; not exactly. Jackie and Jesse still feed him and muck out his stall. But the rest is up to me, and I like it. By the time Susan returns ten days later, I'm wrapping Frank's legs like a pro.

As the temperature drops and the first snow arrives, I experience winter in a whole new way, which, for a New Hampshire native, is really saying something. Iced-over water buckets and gnarled, rutted walkways, skating rink driveways and frozen-shut barn doors are but a few of the joys of the season. One morning after an ice storm, several of us slide down the steep driveway on our bottoms rather than attempting to negotiate it on foot. Many days it's so cold I can't bear to remove Clara's blankets. Instead of riding, we spend quality time.

One Sunday, after several hours of watching a dressage clinic in an unheated arena at a neighboring farm, I go directly to the nearest sporting goods store to buy long underwear and wool socks. No matter what I wear, though, the cold somehow seeps into my bones in a way that it never has before. Now that I'm no longer a child, no longer immune to the cold, I become a fan of down slippers, wool comforters, and crackling fires.

A week later, I wake up to near-blizzard conditions and pad downstairs to find Mark already outside with Jake; Mark shoveling, Jake chasing each shovelful of snow and eating as much of it as possible. I put my down coat on over my sweatpants and slide my bare feet into boots to join them. "Tell me you're not going to the barn today," Mark says worriedly.

"Not if this keeps up. Is it supposed to snow all day?"

"It kinda looks that way."

"Then no, I guess I won't be going."

Back inside, I make us a big breakfast: grapefruit, bacon, eggs, and toast. I'm just warming to the novelty of staying indoors all day when I hear a bonk like the sound of a bird hitting the living room window.

I hurry to look. In lieu of a bird, I'm surprised—happily so—to find my neighbor, Claire, up to her knees in our snow-covered yard, a devilish grin on her face. I'd wondered if I might have a bit more in common with Claire than I did with the other moms on the street, because she'd worked for a New York publishing house before her two kids came along. Now was my chance to find out. Her next snowball hits the window just as her six-month-old Cockapoo leaps in the air only to disappear again inside a deep drift of snow.

I glance over at Mark, who's reading the *New York Times* at the dining room table, still littered with our breakfast dishes.

"Go ahead," he says. "Take the dog. I'll clean up."

So I put on my coat and fasten Jake's collar and the four of us romp in the snow till the dogs are worn out and Claire and I can no longer feel our feet. I then invite them in for hot chocolate and dog treats before they head back up the street. It's a first for Claire and me, and I'm pleased. Here's hoping it will be the first of many.

NOW THAT RIDING OUTDOORS is no longer an option, the indoor ring at Oakwood doesn't feel quite so spacious. Traffic is heavy, collisions inevitable. I consider myself lucky to be riding Clarabelle, who takes the occasional pileup in stride as she does almost everything else.

The more I'm with her, the more I'm struck by the differences between her and Frank: their likes and dislikes, their ways of going, strengths and weaknesses, fears, all are different. Frank is a wreck during windstorms, having once had a portion of the roof peeled off over his head when a tornado touched down years ago. Although that very rarely happens in Connecticut, Frank isn't about to be caught by surprise in the unlikely event it should happen again.

Clarabelle likes a good gallop, and once she's reached her cruising speed, she doesn't much like to stop. She still goes into season beginning in early spring. Unlike some mares, she shows no signs of irritability toward people when she's in heat, but geldings are another story. She has no use for them whatsoever, and when they jostle one another on the trail to get near her, they're liable to get a hoof in the face.

I start picking up bits and pieces of the other horses' quirks. They all seem to have them. Taffy is terrified of cowboy hats. Sampson will do anything for a banana. Limelight, a rescue, is a biter—no doubt the result of having been abused—and Babe kicks out when other horses pass too close to her. The more I learn, the more the horses are thrown into sharp relief, each and every one a distinct character.

Although I still consider Frank my main squeeze, I don't realize how attached I've become to the mare until spring arrives and I overhear her owner telling another boarder that come June, he and his wife are retiring to Florida and taking Clarabelle with them.

And with that, just like that, I find myself dreading the summer. I worry about how Clara will do down in Florida, what with the heat and the bugs. I also hate the thought of her having no one to baby her, no one to spoil her with treats or fuss over her the way I have, as opposed to her owner, who often speaks to her harshly and whacks her endlessly with his crop.

The rest of the spring races by in a blur, the way time tends to pass when you don't want it to. Shortly before Clara is due to head south, Mark makes a rare guest appearance at the barn to take pictures of me riding her—his idea—so I'll have something to remember her by.

After our photo session, I hop off Clara and hand Mark the reins. "Could you hold her for me for a minute? I need to run to the john." He looks at me wide-eyed, consenting only after I've reassured him she won't do anything besides stand there. Proficient as he is at so many things, from editing stories to rewiring our house, it's rare to see him out of his element, rarer still for me to be the one in the know. I must say, I enjoy the novelty.

On my last day with Clara, I take her for one final ride through the neighborhood, then spend an entire afternoon shampooing every speck of dirt from her coat, conditioning her mane and tail, and polishing her hooves. God only knows how she'll look after forty-eight hours on the road, but I'll be damned if she's boarding the trailer for Florida looking anything less than her best.

AUGUST 1996

"Have you looked at him yet?" Missy wants to know. She means the horse Jackie brought in as a prospect for another student, a six-year-old Thoroughbred that gained instant notoriety among the boarders for having dragged his two male handlers across our indoor ring on their stomachs.

"No," I reply, "and I'm not going to."

"Why not?"

I shrug. "What's the point? Jackie's taking him back."

Although true enough, it's a half-hearted excuse and both of us know it. As prospective horse owners, Missy and I are supposed to be training our eyes to detect conformational flaws: the ewe necks, parrot mouths, long backs, and other physical imperfections that can detract from a horse's dressage performance. The more horses we look at, the better we'll get at spotting their faults.

The same is true of riders. With Clarabelle gone, I've had two months to sit around and watch other women ride. As a result, I've become much more discerning. I can tell when a rider is sinking too much into her seat bones, relying too heavily on her hands, or failing to adequately open her hip joint.

I've learned other things, too, over the course of this long, horseless summer: how to muck out a stall; take apart, clean, and reassemble a bridle; poultice a hoof and draw out an abscess. I can take a horse's temperature and check the vitals, clean a sheath and shorten a mane; give an intramuscular injection and dispense oral meds in a dose syringe so that they end up (mostly) in the horse and not all over me.

All summer long back on Hickory Lane, babies and toddlers were everywhere I looked, splashing in wading pools, crawling and scooting through wet grass in damp, sagging diapers. Although I often felt at loose ends without a horse to ride, hanging out at the barn still beat hanging out on my street, especially with my niece and nephew a continent away.

Mark was busy most weekends taking the sailing lessons I got him for Christmas, my attempt to give him something of his own to do while I was off at the barn. So far, so good. He still seems quite taken with this new pursuit.

I've made an effort not to be quite so quick to race into the house at the first sight of a stroller. But just as I was becoming more comfortable around my neighbors, another mini baby boom began. This will be Jenny's second and Nancy's third. Both are sporting visible baby bumps, and I'm backsliding.

"I just wish they'd hurry up and be done already," I complain to my sister over the phone. "But no, they just keep churning them out. Like the world needs more people."

"Try not to take it so personally," Debbie says. "I'm sure they're not doing it to aggravate you."

"How would *you* know?" I grumble. "You're 3,000 miles away." (Far be it for me to pass up a chance to throw that one back in her face.)

Along with everything else I learned at the barn while evading my neighbors over the summer, I also got a firsthand look at two of the leading killers of horses: colic and laminitis. Colic is severe abdominal pain that can have any number of sources, among them: an intestinal blockage caused by impaction of grain, hay, or grass; a twisting of the small intestine or colon that can cut off the blood supply; large numbers of worms that can cause blockages and ruptures of the small intestine; and a host of other conditions, including ulcers.

Signs of colic in a horse include pawing or scraping, pacing, groaning, turning the head toward the stomach and hindquarters, trying to bite or nip the stomach, repeatedly lying down and getting up again, failure to pass manure, and excess salivation. The sight of a severely colicky horse is something you never forget.

Laminitis is a mysterious disease that disrupts blood flow to the laminae, the tiny interlocking fingers that suspend the coffin bone in the horse's foot. Without the flow of blood to deliver oxygen and nutrients to these tissues, the laminae die and the system breaks down. The coffin bone becomes detached from the hoof wall. It then rotates and sinks, a horribly painful condition known as founder.

Common signs of laminitis include heat in the front feet and a pounding pulse in the arteries that supply them; lameness and a painful, shuffling gait; anxiety; an increase in body temperature; sweating and trembling.

A foundering horse also assumes a telltale stance, shifting its weight to its back legs with its front legs extended, precisely the way Frank has been standing for days now.

At first, Susan blamed a recent shoeing for the soreness. "I think the farrier may have taken a little too much off his toe," she said, when I arrived at the barn expecting to see him tacked up for a lesson and found her hand-walking him slowly instead.

We cold-hosed his feet and dosed him with an anti-inflammatory, but instead of getting better, he became increasingly reluctant to move. We switched from cold water to ice, bags and bags of it, gently piled on top of his front feet, which we placed in a couple of rubber feed tubs.

After a few days of this failed to turn things around, it became increasingly apparent that there was more going on than mere foot soreness; just how much more was still up for debate.

"He should start to feel better once his feet grow out a bit," Susan kept saying, though each time she said it, I couldn't help but notice how quiet it suddenly got in the barn.

I finally buttonhole Jackie in the tack room early one morning before Susan arrives. "Would you please tell me what's going on with Frank?"

Instead, she just stands there and looks at me wordlessly until I realize I already know. I feel the hot prick of fresh tears welling up in my eyes, so I turn and walk out.

Jackie catches up with me behind the barn, where I'm sitting on a bench, trying without much luck to compose myself.

"I'm really sorry," she says.

I nod wordlessly; it's a minute or two before I can ask her the question, the one I've been dreading for days. "Will he have to be put down?"

"Yes."

I'm crying again, so once more I nod rather than try to reply.

"I know this is hard. But believe me, he isn't the right horse for you," Jackie says. "He never was."

And although that's beside the point, the hell of it is I'll never get the chance to prove her wrong.

Regardless, I'm not about to abandon Frank, though a part of me wants nothing more than to turn away from the panic in his eyes, as he struggles to shift his weight, again and again, in a futile search for a position that doesn't hurt.

And that is the real reason I don't want to look at the new horse with Missy. I am finished with horses and the heartbreak that comes with them. I want no more to do with an animal that can die from a stomachache, a broken bone, or a mouthful of yew leaves.

"Oh, come on," Missy says. "Aren't you even curious?"

I shrug my sagging shoulders and drop my eyes to inspect my boots. I don't trust myself to speak, not even to tell Missy no. If I open my mouth at all, I'm afraid I will sob. So I let her take me by the arm and lead me over to the stall on the far side of the indoor, the one I've avoided for the past couple of days, ever since the new prospect arrived.

As we approach, I catch a glimpse of his chestnut rump as he stands there with his back to us, wedging his face into the far corner, as if to avoid human contact. Through the bars on his door he looks smaller than his advertised height of 16.2 hands (five feet five inches at the withers), and scrawny besides. He swings his head around and we eye each other warily. We blink. I turn to Missy and shrug. "Meh."

And that's the end of that until late afternoon, when I hear myself mention to Jackie that the new horse in the back stall looks miserable.

She frowns at me. "Miserable how?"

"I don't know, kind of lonely. He looks lost."

Jackie ponders this for a minute as she tacks up her final horse of the day. I check out the pile of bridles from the horses she's already ridden; I count six. And I know from having watched her that she'll ride this last one every bit as long and as hard as the first.

"I'm not going to have time to bring him back till next week," she says, slipping the bit into the mouth of Horse #7. "Maybe I'll ask Karen to sit on him. As long as he's here, he might as well be learning something."

"Good idea."

Later that week, unable to sleep, I make an early morning visit to pack Frank's burning feet in fresh ice and bump into Karen, one of Jackie's more advanced students, who's leaving as I'm arriving.

She says the new horse is doing very well, green but eager. "He's really cute. You ought to come up early tomorrow and watch."

I glance at my watch: barely 7:00 AM. "Just what do you consider early?"

Karen laughs. "How's 6:00?"

It's too damn early, but I tell myself I'll just take a peek. I want to check on Frank anyway, so I go, and I have to agree. The horse *is* cute. Then Karen says, "Come a little earlier tomorrow and you can groom him for me."

Now *that*, I tell myself, is where I draw the line. I will not put my hands on this horse. What begins innocently enough with a brush and a hoof pick ends with heartache and burning feet packed in ice.

That night, I decide not to set my alarm. If I wake up on my own, I'll consider going to the barn and grooming the new horse. If I sleep past 5:30, the choice will have been made for me.

I never even consider the third possibility: that I won't sleep at all. I lie awake for hours worrying about Frank.

There's a growing consensus among the boarders that he should be put down, and soon. There's no doubt he's suffering. And with his coffin bone beginning to rotate and sink, the pain will only get worse.

I can see the anguish in Susan's eyes as she tends to her patient; I can see her denial as well. I know from Missy that a delegation is planning to accost Susan within the next day or two to pressure her to let him go. I know they're right, but I also know Susan's not ready to give up on him. And until she is, neither will I.

Because I'm already wide awake when 5:00 AM rolls around, I figure I might as well get up. I arrive at the barn before sunrise, just as the animals are coming to life. I walk in to a chorus of nickering, the soft, guttural sound a horse makes when greeting a friend; the rhythmic snores of the ones still asleep in the cozy security of their stalls; the slight groans of the newly awakened as they struggle to their feet.

I stop by Frank's stall to dispense a few carrots and give his sweaty neck a reassuring rub. "I'll be back in a little while," I whisper, avoiding his gaze lest I look into his eyes and see only pain. Given the depth of my attachment after only a year, I can just about imagine how bad Susan must feel.

The new horse is still in the stall on the far side of the indoor, a.k.a. Siberia, out of range for my human ears. I cross the ring in the dark and toss a handful of grain into his feed bucket. He'll eat the rest of his breakfast later. A horse needs an hour to digest a grain meal before he can safely be worked. The handful is just enough to reassure him he's not been forgotten.

A few minutes later, after I've checked on Frank again and fed the others, I return to slip on the Thoroughbred's halter and clip on a lead rope. He stands quietly while I do this, though I can see by the tilt of his ears that he's unsure. He doesn't know me, and he doesn't know what I want with him. I talk to him in soothing tones as I lead him across the indoor and cross tie him on the aisle.

I can see the others checking him out while they eat, the dark silhouettes of their heads rising and falling between bites. It's a little before 6:00 when I start with his hooves, sliding my hand down his left foreleg, gently squeezing the tendons above the pastern. Obediently, he lifts his foot and lets me hold it as I pry dirt, stones, and manure out with a hoof pick.

I see nothing remarkable as I clean all four feet, and I'm glad he's well-mannered and willing. Animals whose primary defense is to run away tend to be very protective of their feet.

Next, I slip on a grooming mitt and move my hand in small circles along his body to loosen the dirt, which I then flick away with a stiff dandy brush. I keep my touch light and watch for signs of discomfort or defensiveness—pinned ears, a swishing tail, a raised foot—but he stands stoically throughout. His tail, rather sparse and badly tangled, can wait. I comb his too-long mane and the scruffy forelock that falls over his face. And with that, his neutral expression finally changes to that of a rebellious teenager having his hair combed against his will.

"You don't like that, do you?" I murmur, and reach up to stroke one of his ears. He ducks his head as far as the cross ties will allow, and I immediately drop my hand. The placement of a horse's eyes, on either side of his head, allows for optimal peripheral vision, but there's also a downside: blind spots. Horses have two, one directly in front of them, the other directly behind. I may have inadvertently moved into one of his. "I won't touch them again, I promise. At least, I won't do it today."

I pick up a soft body brush and smooth away the last of the dirt brought to the surface by the currycomb. I'm brushing his legs when I notice the scars: a jagged smile below the right knee, the kind a young child with a crayon might draw, and a long vertical stripe with little treelike branches along the cannon bone on his right hind.

"Oh, my God," I murmur, tracing them with my finger. "What on earth happened to you?"

"He was kicked as a yearling," Jackie tells me later. "Then he went through barbed wire. That one took a year to heal."

Accident prone, I think. *Wonderful.*

I'm curious about his owner, a woman with a Thoroughbred breeding farm in upstate New York, who opted to bring home a horse that was unable to earn his keep on the racetrack or in the breeding shed. "Do you know why she kept him?"

Jackie shrugs. "She just liked him, I guess."

"I like him, too."

I come back the next day and the day after that to groom him before his workouts, telling myself that he needs a familiar face in order to feel a bit more secure in this strange new place. In truth, I need him every bit as much as he needs me, now that Susan has agreed to put an end to Frank's suffering. The vet is coming Friday night to put him down.

In a show of solidarity the night before, a few of us take Susan out for a couple of rounds of tearful drinking. I offer to be there with her on Friday. To my enormous relief, she declines. "The first horse you see put down shouldn't be a horse that you love," she says.

So I stay home the next day with a knot in my stomach, alternately pacing and watching the clock. I can't decide whether to cry or not; the fact that I'm debating seems to point to not crying. That settled, I proceed to bawl like a baby. I arrange to have flowers sent to Susan, along with the one bit of scripture I know that seems comforting and right: Psalm 30:5. "Weeping may endure for a night, but joy cometh in the morning."

I then fall into a deep, dreamless sleep for the first time in more than a week.

four

SEPTEMBER 1996

I WAKE UP THE NEXT MORNING with a vague sense of dread that takes only seconds to sharpen into grief. Frank is gone and I'm about to face his empty stall for the first time. I can only hope that he went peacefully, and that Susan is doing okay.

Thank God for the Thoroughbred bobbing his head to greet me forty-five minutes later, letting out a nicker that's part good-to-see-ya, part where-the-hell-have-you-been?

I open his door to give him his handful of grain and he noses around in my pocket, locating the carrot. He pulls it out and holds it in his lips like a stogie, not quite daring to bite into it. "Go ahead," I tell him. "I brought it for you."

I'm currying his withers on the aisle a few minutes later when he suddenly extends his neck, jutting his nose in the air. I put down the currycomb and switch to my finger-nails, scratching his withers, the bony bump at the top of the shoulder where his neck meets his body. He stretches even taller. I've discovered an itchy spot. I scratch and scratch till my hand starts to cramp.

His responsiveness pleases me. Karen may be his rider, but as his groom, I'm becoming his friend—so much so that a couple of days later, when Jackie mentions she has a free afternoon coming up to return him to his owner, I feel a pang nearly as sharp as the one I feel passing Frank's empty stall.

"I thought you were considering having him stay." It comes out like a whimper. I'm embarrassed, but I have to speak up for him. If I don't, who will?

"Well, I brought him in as an eventing prospect," she says, referring to the equestrian triathlon of show jumping, cross country, and dressage. "He's clearly not that."

She pauses before tightening the girth on a boarder's horse. "But maybe he'd be a good horse for you."

"Really?"

"Let me hop on him," she says. "I can't do it today, but I could probably work him in tomorrow. Just . . . don't get your hopes up."

"I won't." But of course it is too late already. I have plugged this horse into the empty socket of my heart, where he fits more or less perfectly. And with that—just like that—I'm suddenly back in business, ignoring all the advice I've been given about how to shop for and buy my first horse: *Don't get the first one you look at. Take your time. Try out as many as possible.* All of it makes sense. And all of it runs counter to the plan taking shape in my head.

When I get home that afternoon, I take a hot shower, then head over to my neighbor Katie's house four doors down. I need to pay her oldest for some gift wrap I've ordered as part of a fund-raiser for his grammar school. It's an errand I've been putting off for weeks, Katie being the queen of the Hickory Lane moms and, therefore, the most intimidating by virtue of having had the most children (four).

But somehow, the mere prospect of possibly owning this horse gives me the confidence boost I need to finally take care of this unfinished business.

I knock on Katie's door several times before it finally opens to reveal a scene of pure domestic chaos: one kid is yelling, another one's crying, and the other two are pummeling each other with their fists. "I'd invite you in," Katie says, "but as you can see, we're not exactly ready for prime time."

With the sweep of a hand, she acknowledges the bedlam behind her. "This is probably your worst nightmare, huh?"

For a moment, I say nothing as I gauge the dimensions of the yawning chasm between her assumption and my reality. Then, like an infertile Evel Knievel, I give it full throttle and aim for the other side. "No, actually, my worst nightmare was the years I spent having infertility treatments, surgeries, and miscarriages trying to get what you have."

Katie stands there gaping at me as I perform a quick auto-scan to determine whether anything's broken. Hard to say. My cheeks flush a deep scarlet as I mumble an apology. "I don't know where that came from. I'm sorry." I drop the money on the hall table and flee, leaving her standing there with her mouth open.

Home again. With Mark away on a business trip, I seek teary refuge in fur, wrapping my arms around Jake's neck as his tail sweeps the floor, his perfect face puckered with doggy concern. "I don't know what's wrong with me," I tell him. "I thought I was over this, but it still hurts. Thank God I have you."

At that, he flashes his big, toothy trademark Lab grin, the one that never fails to make me grin back. I give him a kiss on the top of his head and tell him that he's my best boy.

I'm still sniffling and smiling as I get up off the floor to answer the phone. "Maybe that's Daddy," I say.

It isn't; it's Katie. "What are you doing tonight?"

"Uh, I don't know. Just hanging out, I guess. Mark's away, so——"

"Good. I'm bringing dinner. See you at eight."

I hang up and shrug my shoulders at Jake. "Looks like we're having company." He tips his head and gives me his puzzled look, the one with his lower lip stuck to his bottom teeth.

"I don't know, either. But I guess we'll find out at eight."

As promised, Katie shows up that evening with a bottle of good Champagne, a loaf of French bread, a wedge of brie, and a basket of strawberries. I get out the good glasses, a cheese board, and a couple of plates as she opens the bottle. With the Champagne poured, the bread cut, and the berries rinsed, she settles herself on the sofa and looks at me expectantly.

"I want to hear the whole story," she says, "soup to nuts."

"The nuts weren't the problem. Mark checked out fine."

She lets loose a big honking laugh and I start to relax for the first time all day. I begin at the beginning and go through the whole sordid tale, test by test, surgery by surgery, and miscarriage by miscarriage. By the time I get to the part about hiding in my house, the bottle is empty.

I fetch another. "What the hell," I say, "it's not like you're driving." And we continue to yak until midnight, not only about infertility, but about families in general, husbands, our street, kids and dogs, horses, sisters and moms. Speaking of moms, I learn that Katie lost hers when she was just twenty-one. She proceeded to give birth to four kids in seven years. So much for the perfect life I'd ascribed to her.

She hadn't a clue about my battle with infertility. Now it's my turn to be shocked. Although come to think of it, why would she? I haven't exactly been very forthcoming.

"I got that you were avoiding me, but I didn't know why," she says. "I thought maybe you just didn't like me. I can't imagine what it must be like for you to live on this street."

"It's been hard," I reply. "It's a great street in so many ways, and I really do love my house. But there've been times when I've wished the wind would just pick it up and set it down someplace—*anyplace*—else."

By the time we say goodnight, I feel buzzed, drained, and relieved, in roughly that order.

I realize there's no such thing as a quick fix, and I'm sure I will still have bad days. But at least I won't feel quite so misunderstood. I wish we'd done this a long time ago.

⋆₊⁺

THE NEXT MORNING, I'm as nervous as a stage mother on opening night as I wait for Jackie to audition my guy. I groom him and tack him up, whispering instructions all the while: *Do your best. Do whatever she asks. Don't be nervous.* Undoubtedly, though, I'm telegraphing my own jitters with every touch.

The minute I hand him over, I try to shake it all off so I can watch with a somewhat open mind. He looks small and unsure of himself next to six-foot-tall Jackie, but I know he's in excellent hands.

She doesn't expect him to know very much, certainly not after a week. He just has to demonstrate that he has a good attitude. He just has to show her his willingness to learn.

She swings her right leg over his back and lowers herself onto the saddle, then gives him a friendly pat on the neck. She leaves her reins long and nudges him into a walk, encouraging him to lengthen his stride. After a few minutes of this, she begins to gather up the reins, using her legs to push him into the bridle.

He immediately rounds his neck and bends from the poll, the first vertebra just behind his ears. Aligned with the flow of energy that travels from his haunches through his spine, he maintains this posture as Jackie picks up a posting trot. He looks great with Jackie on him, but so would a basset hound. So would a cow.

She trots him briskly around the indoor, changing direction after a few minutes. He is concentrating intently, listening closely and attentively for her aids, evident from the way his ears swivel back toward his rider. With her outside leg behind the girth, she asks him to canter, and that's where it all falls apart. He trots faster, then trips, then recovers, then scrambles. I wonder if he has balance issues, which would not be surprising, given his lack of training.

Before I have a chance to process all this, Jackie halts and dismounts. "Okay, your turn."

"Huh?"

"I can't tell you to buy him without seeing you on him."

"What, now?" Suddenly, my mouth is Death Valley. I curse my choice of clothing. I should never have shown up in britches and boots. Why the hell didn't I wear stilettos?

"Come on. Let's see."

I walk him back to the mounting block in the corner; in his eagerness, he sets off at a brisk pace before I can shorten the stirrups. "Make him wait," Jackie says. I close my fingers on the reins, asking him to halt so I can get myself together. Then I look to Jackie for my next move.

"Walk him on a long rein. Relax. Be a passenger for a minute."

I try. Way too hard. I'm stiff as a board, too nervous to go with his motion. Too much is riding on this ride. Then there's Frank. How can I be so disloyal? How can I consider buying another horse just hours after his death?

"Stop a minute," Jackie says.

We halt. I can't even look at her. I feel miserable.

"We're not going to decide today, so don't panic. Take a deep breath and hold it, then let it out slowly."

I glance at myself in the mirrors—a fixture in indoor dressage rings—and see my tense, worried face, stiff arms and back. I take a deep breath, then another.

"Ready now?"

I nod.

We set off at a walk, and though I have neither Jackie's long legs nor her expert feel, I can sense what I do have: the trust of this horse. He and I are in this together.

I pick up a posting trot and after watching us for a few minutes, Jackie stops us again. "I definitely wouldn't want to see you on anything bigger," she says. "His canter obviously needs work, but I don't need to see you canter him to tell you to buy him."

My heart is leaping about like a trout in my chest and I'm patting the horse's neck with both hands.

"Why don't we do another lesson on Saturday and see how you do. We'll go from there."

I nod, too overwhelmed to speak. I hop off and lead the horse—possibly *my* horse—back to the barn for his treats.

* * *

DRIVING HOME, I tell myself to calm down. He's not mine and he may never be. We still have another lesson to go, and he'll need to be checked out from head to tail by our fastidious barn vet. I shudder to think of all the faults he could find.

The next day, when Mark returns from his business trip, I put on my best (read: none too good) poker face. "Okay, what's going on?" he asks.

"I rode him," I whisper, not quite daring to say it out loud. "Jackie's giving me a lesson on him next Saturday, and if all goes well, maybe . . ."

"Hey, that's great!"

The rest of the week is a nauseating write-off as I ping-pong between grief over Frank and giddiness over the Thoroughbred, an all-too-familiar state from years of bouncing back and forth between short-lived pregnancies and the inevitable miscarriages.

I feel sorry for my rock-steady husband, who's doing his best to hang on, though it's not like he hasn't ridden this particular roller coaster before.

Friday night I lie awake in anticipation of Saturday's lesson. "Can't sleep, huh?" Mark asks, after about the tenth time I rearrange my pillows and sigh heavily.

"I'm a train wreck," I say. "I keep going back and forth between what if it doesn't work out and what if it does."

He turns on his side to face me. "I thought you wanted it to work out."

"I *do*. I'm just nervous. There's so much I don't know about owning a horse. What if I'm not any good at it?"

"I'm sure you'll learn, just like everyone else," he says. "No one's born knowing."

Right. It just seems that way. The next morning, with Mark and Susan both looking on with crossed fingers, my lesson goes even better than I'd dared hope. We make the vet appointment for the following Tuesday, when I duck out of work to go get the horse ready, thanking God that my editor is also an animal lover.

I curry the horse from top to bottom, brushing away all the dirt and loose hair. I comb his mane, tail, and forelock, and pick the pebbles and dirt from his hooves, finishing with a soft body brush that sweeps away the last of the dullness. His chestnut coat shines.

Through it all he maintains a sense of decorum, as if he *knows* something special and important is about to take place. There's no nosing around in my pockets, no begging for treats, no pawing the floor. He stays respectful even as I wipe out his ears.

The vet arrives, wearing his usual dour expression, and I nervously introduce him to my prospect. "Don't feel bad when he doesn't say anything nice," Jackie has warned me. "He never does. And be prepared for him to find flaws. There's no such thing as a perfect horse. Just remember it's nothing personal."

To our mutual amazement, however, he starts complimenting the gelding almost immediately. "Nice and quiet, isn't he," he says as he begins his assessment. "Are you sure he's a Thoroughbred?"

"Yup," Jackie says with a grin. "He's a horse for Nancy to learn on."

The vet pats his neck. "Well, if I were looking for a horse to learn on, I'd love to find something as quiet as this."

I shoot Jackie a look, sending her a telepathic message not to ruin the moment by describing the horse's tumultuous arrival, but I needn't have worried. She says nothing.

For the next forty-five minutes, the vet probes and palpates. He listens to the horse's heart and lungs. He peers into eyes, assesses teeth, and feels limbs. He takes X-rays of the horse's lower legs, tests his hooves for sensitivity, and draws blood, all the while marveling at his even temperament and his soft, kind eye.

We then saddle him up so the vet can watch him go. Having ridden him all of twice, I've asked Jackie to do the honors. The vet begins with a flexion test, in which he holds the horse's left front leg in a flexed position, closing the joint angles for a minute or so. The horse is then trotted off while the vet evaluates the first few strides for any unevenness indicative of lameness. The test is repeated for each remaining leg.

Some vets dispute the value of flexion tests as reliable predictors of soundness, though ours obviously isn't among them. There's a slight issue with the horse's right front; not a deal-breaker, fortunately, but enough to lower the horse's rating from "sound" to "serviceably sound." The vet takes X-rays of the right front foot, then packs up his equipment and leaves.

I take the horse back into the indoor and hand-walk him, less out of necessity than the sheer joy of walking beside him. "He really, really liked you," I tell him. "And he doesn't like *anyone*."

He stops and wipes his mouth on my shoulder, leaving a trail of green slime on my new slate-blue sweater. So much for decorum. He then looks at me as if to say, *Now what?*

I give his withers a friendly scratch.

"Now we wait."

I'm at my desk the next morning, halfheartedly trying to write a lead, when the phone rings and I pounce. It's Jackie with the results of the X-rays. The first words out of her mouth are, "Don't cry."

My heart does a nose dive, but I bite my lip and obey. "Okay," I say. "Hit me."

The vet's X-rays of the horse's right front foot show a spur on the navicular bone, a bone often implicated in front-foot lameness. In this case, it may never cause a problem. Then again, the horse could break down in a week.

"What does he think I should do?"

"His advice was to pound the hell out of him, ride him hard—ride him on pavement—and see whether or not he holds up."

This immediately strikes me as a terrible idea. "I need to think. Let me get back to you."

I mull over his recommendation. Paying for expert advice only to ignore it is foolhardy. Then again, why pound the horse if that's not how I'm planning to use him? That's asking for trouble, and unsportsmanlike besides.

The purchase price is fairly negligible; at $6,500, it's mostly commissions for Jackie and the dealer who represents the breeder. Obviously, the owner isn't looking for a big payday so much as a good home for her horse. I can't imagine she'd object to me leasing him for a couple of months and working him normally, not with an eye toward destroying him. If he holds up, I'll pay her the balance. If not, she can keep the lease payments.

I run this by Mark first, taking advantage of his innate sense of fair play and the fact that he wants this to work out every bit as much as I do. Once he's signed on to my plan, I lay it out for Jackie the next morning. Like Mark, she looks greatly relieved. "Good," she says. "Perfect."

"One other thing," I add. "He needs a better name." True Tone, his registered racing name, the name that he came with, sounds vaguely reminiscent of True Value® paint.

Jackie agrees. "I've been calling him Tony, just to call him something."

I consider "Tony" for a minute. Nope. "I'm going to call him Eli," I announce, without a clue where that name came from. Somehow, it just popped right out. "What do you think?"

"Eli. I love it!" She turns to the barn manager. "Jesse," she says, "take Eli and turn him out in the middle paddock."

five

OCTOBER 1996

MUCH TO MY RELIEF, the seller agrees to my terms. The first thing I notice during this provisional ownership period is that I'm suddenly trusted to do favors: "Could you hold my horse for a minute?" "Will you be here tomorrow? Could you hand-walk my mare?" "Could you spare a little duct tape? I can't find mine."

Even Jesse, the ice queen, seems to thaw out a bit, at least to the point of acknowledging my comings and goings with a curt little nod.

With two exceptions—Susan's husband and a boy not yet old enough to drive—Jackie's current boarders are all female, not surprising for a sport increasingly dominated by women. What does surprise me, though, is how many of us are middle-aged.

Edith, the cranky teacher I met that first day, is in her mid-sixties and still saddling up her Welsh pony, White

Lightning, three or four times a week. Susan, in her late forties, has decided to buy a young warmblood, the cross of hot-blooded Thoroughbred and cold-blooded draft horse favored by more and more dressage riders these days. Susan plans to train him herself.

The fact that we're all still nursing our childhood crushes decades later strikes me as a curious thing, especially given the realities of equestrian sports. For the most part, we're not experts, and we're probably never going to be; what we're more likely to be, sooner or later, is injured. Even so, our enthusiasm remains undimmed.

That owning a horse in suburban Connecticut on the eve of the new millennium is a privilege seems obvious enough on a crisp autumn morning or a balmy spring afternoon; less so on a frigid February morning when drinking water freezes in buckets and sheets of ice cover the ground.

On such days, owning a horse could conceivably feel like a hardship. A self-imposed one to be sure, but a hardship nonetheless.

I can't wait.

I make my first investment in horse apparel even before I own the horse: a turnout sheet for rainy days and cool nights in a hunter green shade that complements his chestnut coat. I can see that Eli's going to need more as the temperature drops, but technically he won't be mine until November, and that's assuming the trial period goes well for us.

Still, mine or not, he's beginning to look underdressed on these chilly October mornings. I turn right around and sink some serious bucks into a Rambo turnout, $350 worth of tough love in heavy-duty, waterproof ballistic nylon.

"Let's face it," I overhear Missy saying to Susan, "that horse isn't going anywhere."

In the ring, just as we're getting more comfortable with each other, I discover what's behind the mild-mannered temperament I've been bragging about. Beneath Eli's placid exterior lurks a big spook. I first encounter it indoors, midway through a lesson in which I am concentrating so hard that I don't even hear the noise that turns him into a rocket. One minute we're trotting a fifteen-meter circle; the next, we're at the opposite end of the ring, Eli flying and me shouting: "Shit, Jackie! Shit!"

Then she's shouting, too: "SIT BACK!" How many times does she say it before it sinks in and I finally do it? Only then do I realize how far forward I'm leaning in response to our sudden flight. The minute I heed Jackie's instruction, Eli miraculously comes right back under me, though I wonder how in the heat of the moment I'm going to remember to sit myself back.

I also can't help but wonder how many times over the course of our partnership such shenanigans will be repeated, and to what end. This time, at least, I stay on. Still, I'm rattled. It could just as easily have gone the other way, and nearly did.

"What the hell was that?" I ask as I walk him in circles, waiting for our heart rates to slow. "What set him off?"

"A truck backfired," Jackie says.

"You're kidding. I didn't even hear it."

"Yeah, I could tell."

An hour later, when we're back on the aisle, I stop brushing him for a moment to plumb the depths of his big, soft brown eyes. "Okay this time," I tell him. "No lives were lost, no harm was done. But in the future, you need to cut that shit out. I don't bounce the way I used to."

He plops his chin on my shoulder and burrows his nose under my hair, as in, *Sorry! I'll never do it again!* But it's soon apparent my little speech has gone in one furry ear and out the other.

Running away—from a sudden loud noise or movement, a barking dog, say, or dry leaves rattling in a breeze; an unexpected sight, such as the horse's own sheet or cooler neatly folded and hung on a cross rail; a mud puddle in the outdoor ring; a manhole cover encountered on a trail ride; a bunch of balloons tied to a mailbox for a realtor's open house; an unclaimed newspaper lying at the end of a driveway—is a horse's only reliable defense. Teeth made for tearing and grinding forage are no match for those of a meat-eating predator, and a kick from a back hoof—the last resort of the cornered horse—only tends to endanger the leg to which it's attached.

I *know* this, but the knowledge makes it no less unnerving when Eli shies, spins, or bolts at some imaginary threat. Moreover, I can't help but notice he doesn't seem to do any of these things anywhere near as often when Jackie is riding him. When I mention this to her, she suggests I give him something else to think about besides the folded-up cooler or the unclaimed newspaper.

"Keep him busy," she says.

With what? A coloring book and crayons? His very own laptop?

Of course she means keep him busy with work, as in raise the bar, increase the degree of difficulty. I try. But I'm already at the outer edge of my own capability. And in addition to the spooking, spinning, and skittishness Eli initiates, he also feeds off the antics of all the other horses in the ring with us. I recall with great fondness my months with Saint Clarabelle. She obviously ruined me for life.

Lying awake one night, in lieu of sheep, I count the times I've fallen off horses. I can recall only six, none of which resulted in serious injury. There was the time I slid down a horse's neck into a woodland stream in rural New Hampshire. The time I got dumped in a field in my hometown within three minutes of getting on the horse. The trail ride in New Mexico when I got knocked off by a tree branch. Embarrassing? Very. But dangerous?

I'd yet to break a single bone, not even the time I slid halfway across an outdoor ring in Vermont, slamming my head into a fencepost. Although that was the end of my helmet, my head stayed intact. Even so, the thought of coming off Eli gives me pause. I'm no kid anymore, and he's no pony. It's a long way down from the back of a 16.2-hand horse, especially one that takes off as if from a starting gate.

Before I know it, I'm subjecting Eli to ridiculous parental lectures on such topics as thinking for himself and not giving in to peer pressure. "If Casey jumped off a cliff, would you do it, too?"

"Well, duh. Yeah. I am a herd animal, after all." (I also provide his voice in our little exchanges.)

After a snicker or two from my fellow horsewomen, I forgo the speeches and focus on trying to ride through the spooks, since I can count on them happening with great regularity. So far I stay on, though my form isn't pretty. I'm glad no one is videotaping us.

I have to admit he'd look great in a video, though, with his pretty head and neck, solid chestnut except for the perfect white star on his forehead, and the single white sock on his right hind. He could definitely stand to put on some weight, though work should help take care of that. I look forward to both of us muscling up. Otherwise, the scars on his legs—from the kick and the barbed wire—are the only outward signs of the life he led before fate led him to me.

A couple of weeks later, while cleaning my brush box, I come across a half-written letter to a woman I used to ride with in Vermont, listing all the exemplary traits I was seeking in my search for a horse of my own: "My ideal horse would be an amalgam of all the great horses I've known: bombproof like Clarabelle, sensitive like Frank, sane and sturdy like the school horses of old."

Knowledgeable people have advised me to look around carefully and to ride as many prospects as I can. Excellent advice. I planned to follow it, too, until the scrawny, scarred spook came along.

Is he really the right horse for me? Well, he's young, a good thing. With luck, we could be together for a long time. True, he has a lot to learn, but so do I. We can learn it together. Granted, he's a bit of a handful. At least I won't outgrow him anytime soon.

It would've been nice to have learned how to ride— *really* ride—as a kid, but obviously that ship has sailed. Is it too late now? That's up to me to decide. I could opt out, but haven't I missed out on enough?

It's okay to be scared; every expectant mother is. "The whole time I was pregnant with Sam, I called him The Thing," Claire recently confessed. "I couldn't even think of him as a baby. I knew nothing about babies. I'd never changed a diaper in my life. And then there I was in the delivery room. You bet your ass I was scared."

On the plus side of my pro-and-con ledger, I add not having to push Eli out.

I say a silent good-bye to the things I'm about to give up: clean fingernails, lazy mornings, low mileage, discretionary income, brunch with friends, time to myself.

I dial Mark. "I've decided. I'm going to do it," I say.

"Good for you! I'm putting the Champagne in the fridge," he says. "We can celebrate when you get home."

Then, with an ever-so-slightly-shaking hand, I write the check.

He's mine! Eli is mine.

I bring him into the indoor to tell him the news, pausing to study us in the mirrors along the wall. In many ways, we're an odd couple. I'm short, he's tall. I'm middle-aged, he's a baby. I'm female, he's gelded. It's a fairly long list, but who's counting? Such things don't matter when you're in love.

Once I've made it official, I set out to introduce Eli to friends and relations, colleagues and virtual strangers, unleashing years' worth of pent-up baby lust. I shamelessly send birth announcements, crossing out "It's a girl!" and writing in "It's a gelding!"

My Hickory Lane neighbors, mothers all, make pilgrimages to the barn to take countless pictures and ooh and aah over my new half-ton baby. Amy and Claire, both with fearless young daughters in tow, are our first visitors, followed by Alex, who comes bearing carrots. And others: Mark's parents, one of my sisters-in-law, two of my nieces, colleagues from The Associated Press. Next come my parents, with Totes rubber boots over their shoes, gingerly negotiating the steep driveway to the barn. My father eagerly strokes Eli's neck, while my mother opts to admire him from a safe distance.

Just as the traffic is beginning to slow, my sister comes east for a visit. No sooner are Debbie and Eli introduced than I catch the two of them smooching through the bars on his door, a sight that makes me insanely happy.

Back on my stroller-strewn street, the neighborhood moms tuck dark leggings into tall boots and don formfitting blazers to throw me my "bridle" shower. I cry all the way through it, over everything from the carrot cake to the gifts: buckets and sponges, a hoof pick, a brush, a set of polo wraps, bags of carrots, and jars of molasses cookies.

I can't thank them enough. "I love you guys! Now I have everything I've ever wanted. I feel so blessed."

I feel other things, too: sad and happy, exhilarated and scared; with another's life to nurture and protect, my heart as full as any mother's heart.

six

1997

THE DIFFERENCE BETWEEN LOVING HORSES in the generic sense and owning one very real, very specific horse in the literal sense is trotted out again and again for my edification over the course of my first year with Eli.

Gone are the days when I could simply admire the tint and sheen of his chestnut coat without also inspecting it for signs of the countless fungal and bacterial infections to which horses are prone.

Nor can I afford to refrain from checking the quantity and consistency of the balls of manure nestled in the shavings within his stall, or the evenness of his footfalls as I lead him out onto the concrete aisle at dawn, or any of the countless other indicators of his overall health.

With horses, vigilance is key. I vow to be vigilant.

Even so, little things get by me. A cut too small to see goes untreated, breeds bacteria, and becomes infected; a sharp pebble gets wedged in the underside of his hoof and causes a stone bruise that takes forever to heal. Each time it happens, each time my horse pays the price for my momentary lapse of attention I'm reminded of the children's nursery rhyme about the escalating consequences of a small, careless act:

For want of a nail the shoe was lost.
For want of a shoe the horse was lost.
For want of a horse the rider was lost.
For want of a rider the battle was lost.
For want of a battle the kingdom was lost.
And all for the want of a horseshoe nail.

Like virtually everything else having to do with *Equus caballus*, there's simply no substitute for a practiced eye. Unfortunately, a practiced eye can take years to develop. The good news is that I'm surrounded by them: not only Jackie's, but Karen's, Missy's, and Susan's, to name but a few. Everyone at Oakwood knows far more than I, and though there are times when their input feels wonderfully reassuring, it can also, at times, feel like crap.

It can also feel a lot like open season on me and my lack of experience.

"You're not doing it hard enough," Nicole, a part-time barn staffer, informs me as she sweeps in the aisle where I'm currying my horse.

"Move it forward. That's too far down," says Justine, owner of the white horse across the aisle, as she critiques my saddle placement on Eli's back.

Karen, sizing up the bunch of carrots in my hand: "You're overtreating him again! Not so many."

"Shorten your reins," says a woman from the upper barn whose name I don't even know, as she and her Morgan trot past Eli and me in the crowded indoor ring during prime time on a Wednesday evening.

Clearly, there isn't a boarder here who doesn't feel right at home taking me to task for anything and everything I do with regard to my horse.

Although I can only assume that they're right in their respective assessments, each has a different prescription for how best to correct what I'm doing wrong. As a result, for each and every point taken, I face an annoyed woman demanding to know why I didn't take *hers*.

On the outside, the iconic outline of a horse—*any* horse—is as familiar to me as my dreams. But now that Eli is mine, my responsibility for his well-being needs to be more than skin-deep. The exotic terminology I hear bandied about—*stifle, fetlock, gaskin, pastern*—describes this new equine geography. It's high time I learned it—not only the jargon, but the anatomy to which it refers.

So I do what any horse-crazy sixth-grader might do: I go online and order the Visible Horse, a see-through model for ages ten and up. By piecing together the puzzle of its scaled-down skeleton and vital organs, I hope to develop a more intimate understanding of Eli's innards.

The first thing I notice when the model arrives and I set to work on the skeletal system is how reminiscent of a dinosaur a horse's bone structure appears. The resemblance is downright freaky.

I move on to the flesh-colored plastic pieces that represent the organs: the relatively small stomach that holds just four gallons of food and works best when it's only half full; the enormous lungs that, if their airways were opened out and laid flat on the ground, would occupy a total area equivalent to ten tennis courts; the heart, typically eight and one-half pounds, that can pump thirty to forty liters of blood per minute, compared with the average woman's five liters, the most notable exception being that of the late Secretariat, whose famously outsized heart was estimated to have weighed twenty-two pounds. The English racehorse, Eclipse, had a fourteen-pound heart.

Put them all together—along with the myriad other puzzle pieces, of course—and what you have is essentially a running machine. Organic and elegant, beautiful and efficient, but a running machine nonetheless.

Although he was referring to an office building, American architect Louis Sullivan might as easily have been alluding to the horse when he wrote:

> *It is the pervading law of all things organic and inorganic,*
> *Of all things physical and metaphysical,*
> *Of all things human and all things super-human,*
> *Of all true manifestations of the head,*
> *Of the heart, of the soul,*
> *That the life is recognizable in its expression,*
> *That form ever follows function. This is the law.*

I'll never succeed in memorizing the names of all 205 bones, let alone every muscle, tendon, and ligament, but I now have a far better sense of the architectural underpinnings beneath Eli's majestic exterior.

* * *

ELSEWHERE IN MY LIFE, beyond the boundaries of the barn and its insular universe of horses and women, my sudden ownership at age forty-two of an off-the-track Thoroughbred seems to strike some in my circle of acquaintances as downright wacky, like a plot for an old episode of *I Love Lucy*. A neighbor whose interests lean more toward gardening and golf never asks how "the horse" is doing without sporting a smirk.

My more competitive friends make a point of trying to get me to stay up late, something I'm loath to do in light of my early mornings with Eli. "Oh, come on," they chide. "You can go see him a little later." Occasionally, I cave in to the pressure to have one more drink or stay out another hour, but I almost always pay for it the next morning with a lackluster lesson or a horrendous commute, as opposed to my usual pre-rush-hour breeze.

On a brighter note, Zoe and my other young nieces, Samantha and Rachel, the daughters of Mark's younger brothers, think I'm the coolest aunt who ever lived. I'm soon inundated with an art gallery's worth of crayoned drawings of Eli to prove it. I reciprocate by sending them photos of their handsome four-legged cousin. To them, at least, I'm a relative expert.

Now that I have Eli to talk about, I'm also more at ease around the neighborhood kids, who gaze at his pictures wide-eyed and clamor to know when he'll be coming to live on our street.

To my barn mates, however, I remain a perpetual rookie. And try as I might, I can't seem to prove them wrong.

When Eli develops an abscess, temporarily crippling but nowhere near as serious as it appears, I lose count of the number of times he kicks over the bucket of warm water and Epsom salts in which I am trying to soak his foot to draw it out. Next, a wrestling match ensues as I attempt to coat the foot with salve, cover it with gauze, wrap it in Vetrap™, a kind of gauze that sticks to itself, and finish with a protective layer of duct tape, all without letting the relatively clean foot make contact with the unsanitary barn floor.

These and other routine procedures require multiple limbs to perform: one pair of hands to tend to the abscessed foot and a spare to hold another of his feet off the floor, rendering him immobile. It's a great trick, provided one has three hands.

Some days, I wonder whether Eli's raison d'être is to make me look as inept as possible as often as possible—a fair question, since he never seems to run out of ways.

For all that, there is still something wonderful about having something—some*one*—who's all mine, a commitment nobody can challenge. "I'm sorry I can't do breakfast/come visit/go away for the weekend," I tell my girlfriends/parents/husband. "I can't leave Eli, not when he's sick/hurt/laid up."

"Can't you ask someone else to cover for you just this once?" my friend Alex wants to know, when I beg off on an overnight trip with the girls. The truth is, I probably could. But *I* want to take care of him. Me. Not some barn worker who's being paid by the hour to look after him and two dozen others. Not when he's just beginning to recognize and respond to me as his designated human, his—you should pardon the expression—mom.

It's my choice to be on call for any and all Eli emergencies. The first occurs as Mark and I are returning from seeing a movie. I hit the button on the answering machine and hear the distinctive Australian accent of Milli, one of the weekend barn staffers, and the words "not feeling well." At that, I'm already halfway out the door.

By the time I get there, exceeding the speed limit all the way, Milli is hand-walking an unhappy-looking Eli who emits a pathetic little nicker the minute he sees me. I fly up the aisle and he plops his head on my shoulder.

"He feels hot," I say to Milli.

"His temperature was 103. I gave him some bute," she replies, referring to the anti-inflammatory drug phenylbutazone, commonly given to horses as a pain reliever. "His fever's already starting to come down. I just figured you might want to be here."

"Thanks. You were right, I do."

Within the hour, Eli has brightened, his fever is gone, and he's inhaled the dinner he'd rejected earlier. And though I missed the worst of it, I'm grateful not to have missed the whole thing.

Once, while I was kicking a soccer ball back and forth in my sister's backyard with my then four-year-old tow-headed nephew, he slipped on the wet grass and fell on his bottom. Unhurt but indignant, he picked himself up and ran toward me crying; I knelt in the grass and held out my arms. He then blew right by me and ran straight to my sister, who'd come out of the house and was standing behind me, summoned by that sixth sense mothers have.

That was the exact moment I knew that I wanted a baby. And now, here he is, with his big sweaty head on my shoulder, looking to me to make it all better.

What could be better than that?

₊

EGO ASIDE, at the end of the day none of my inadequacies at horse keeping detract from the stuff that really matters, the moments that are just Eli's and mine. They come along every now and then: the day he watches me hug a girlfriend in greeting and jealously insinuates his head in between us; the morning he responds to my momentary tears of frustration by bringing his luminous brown eye so close to my blue one, I feel the sweep of his chestnut lashes as he peers as if into my soul.

And along with my very public blunders, there are occasional public triumphs as well, like the morning I glance over during a lesson at the normally empty bench in the indoor and see three boarders sitting there attentively watching us as we trot by.

Later, as I'm putting my saddle away in the tack room, I overhear one of the Susans ask Jackie how she could possibly give the same lesson to both of us "when I've been riding for years and Nancy's just a beginner?"

"She's doing it, that's how," Jackie says. I grin like a goon all the way home.

Of course, it doesn't hurt that she rides Eli at the start of each lesson to sharpen him up and make him easier for me. How much easier I have no idea until the day I insist on riding him first.

"Okay, now, maintaining the right bend, push in his haunch to the inside with your left leg," Jackie instructs as Eli and I trot clockwise around the ring. I look at her as though she's grown another head.

"Push in his *what* with my *what?*"

"His haunch with your left leg, behind the girth," she says.

"My left leg barely clears the saddle pad! How's he supposed to feel it?"

"It's up to you to make him respond. Use your spur if he ignores your leg. And if he ignores your spur, give him a tap with your whip," she says.

By the time I manage to push his haunch in far enough to satisfy Jackie, my left leg feels like rubber, my right forearm aches, and Eli and I are both hot and sweaty. "This *can't* be right," I tell Missy later. "Dressage can't possibly be this hard."

She mulls that over for a moment, then: "Did it feel like your leg was about to fall off? Did your back ache and your calf muscles cramp?"

"Yeah!" I reply excitedly. "All those things."

Missy grins. "Yup, you're doing it right."

My aching muscles eventually respond to repeated doses of Advil and soaks in my friend Amy's hot tub, but for the first day or two, I'm unable to pull off my britches and boots without wincing. I can't decide which hurts the worst: my arms, my legs, my torso, or my pride.

Arduous though it is, dressage has its hooks in me right from the start, with its promise of a seamless, harmonious connection between a quiet, balanced rider and her calm, obedient horse. Its timeless principles call for a progression of training that works in tandem with the animal's developing athleticism; hence, there is always room for improvement.

There's also always more for both horse and rider to learn as they work their way up the levels of difficulty from Introductory all the way to Grand Prix, the ultimate test and the one in which riders compete at the Summer Olympics. No need to save a slot for me, guys.

Each segment of a dressage test is scored on a scale of 1 to 10, with 10 being excellent and 0 being a required movement that isn't performed. It says a lot about the discipline that there are four separate scores reserved to indicate degrees of badness: 4 Insufficient; 3 Fairly Bad; 2 Bad; and 1 Very bad.

A horse naturally carries 60 to 65 percent of his weight on his front legs. One of the primary aims of dressage is to bring the horse into better balance by training him to support more of his weight—and his rider's—with his hindquarters, analogous to putting the engine in the back of a car.

A horse that's been trained to carry himself this way is a joy to ride, with smoother, more powerful gaits, improved balance, and a lightness that translates into an elastic feel in the reins; this, as opposed to a horse that's strung out, one that leans on his rider's hands and trips often. A horse that's learned to use his hind end properly is also less likely to develop arthritis and other joint problems from years of carrying too much weight on his front legs.

The same concepts that can be expressed in a paragraph can take years to master, as Eli and I are finding out. Dressage at its best is a buoyant ballet of power and grace that appears effortless; at its worst, it looks a lot like Eli and me as we wrestle over which of us is calling the shots. Unfortunately—for me, anyway—the stronger of us generally wins.

Eli's resistance to doing what I ask when I ask for it—bending his neck to the left, say, or yielding to, rather than pulling against, my hands when I shorten the reins—challenges my ridiculous, hopelessly romantic notions of the cooperative relationship I feel entitled to by virtue of my unfailingly kind and loving treatment of my horse.

Why *wouldn't* he live to please me, the provider of organic carrots and glossy green apples? Why *not* yield to the hand that delivers an endless supply of Mrs. Pastures molasses cookies for horses at $22.95 per five-pound bag?

Because bribery doesn't work with horses. Because a horse is not a dog. Because Eli isn't predator but prey, and if I want him to accept me as his leader, I need to start acting like one. That means riding him with greater authority, a goal that requires a thorough understanding of the herd mentality, which I have, along with strength, timing, and finesse, which I don't.

Despite its difficulty, dressage does give me tantalizing glimpses—fleeting, to be sure—of a kind of perfection that's hard to describe and easy to get hooked on.

Up to now, I had only ridden horses that carried their weight (and mine) on their front ends, horses that hollowed their backs and jutted their chins in the air to evade the bits in their mouths. I'm getting a taste of what comes of working in tandem with a horse, rather than struggling in opposition to one.

On rare occasions, I find I have only to think about asking Eli for something—a transition from walk to trot, say, or a change of rhythm within the trot—for him to oblige me. At such moments, I believe that I have finally found my religion.

I learn that there is something called "feel" that, though it can be developed, cannot be entirely taught, something that Jackie has in spades and that I seem to have not at all. Although in time, maybe, especially if I work hard enough—?

Working hard, it turns out, is not the same thing as *trying* hard, which has a nasty way of turning into trying too hard, as Jackie frequently reminds me not to do. "Easy for you to say," I grumble back, as, dripping with sweat and trembling with muscle fatigue, I slide off my horse and hand over the reins.

Along with being a professional trainer, Jackie is also a very natural rider, that rare individual who can sit on horse after horse and know more or less immediately exactly what each needs from her in order to perform optimally. It's a gift, much like legs that go on and on and on, versus mine, which barely make it to the ground.

Watching Jackie ride Eli, I am the very soul of ambivalence, at once thrilled and crushed to see how much my horse is capable of giving when ridden correctly, that is, not by me.

Missy insists this is good. "The fact that he won't give you what you want unless you ask for it correctly means he'll end up teaching you more than you'd ever learn from riding some schoolmaster."

I wish. A schoolmaster is a highly trained animal that excels at whatever it is that you're trying to learn. An inexperienced or "green" horse like mine is at the opposite end of the spectrum, though a talented rider like Jackie can help him develop a greater understanding of what's being asked of him at specific moments.

Although I see Missy's point, I'm also seeing the downside of the green horse—green rider partnership. Not only do I see it, I feel it, too, never more so than on the day Eli dances around a mud puddle in the outdoor ring and I, with a mighty plop, wind up on my ass in the middle of it.

I pop right back up—I'm not hurt, only mortified— and am treated to the sight of my riderless horse running around the ring willy-nilly, with a hundred bucks' worth of borrowed dressage reins dangling in front of him, waiting to be stepped on. Jackie calmly calls Jesse to come close the gate and plants herself in Eli's path, stopping him cold. Crisis averted.

"Come on, Cowgirl," says my trainer, cupping her man-hands. "Up you go." With some difficulty—I am covered with mud, after all—I step into her hands and heave myself into the saddle. Not pretty, but at least I'm back on.

I'm also relieved to have my first fall from Eli over with, and virtually painless at that. I've been lucky.

I've been lucky at work, too, having managed to sidestep most travel assignments in my first few months of horse ownership in favor of stories that are reachable by shuttle, car, or train.

Even though I've been working, I've made it a point to choose less ambitious stories than usual, having come to regard the last several months as a kind of maternity leave. I realize it can't last forever; I am destined to continue working, after all, with all the juggling and guilt that it entails. I don't yet know how to pull off the balancing act with agility and grace, but it's time I start learning.

No sooner has that thought taken hold in my brain than I get assigned a couple of stories that will take me first to Chicago, then on to the West Coast. I'll be gone a little over a week. Jackie offers to ride Eli at a discounted rate while I'm away, so at least I have the day care problem solved.

Saying good-bye to my horse for a week on the eve of my cross-country trip damn near kills me. I grasp his halter and turn his head toward me for maximum eye contact. "I have to tell you something," I say. "I'm going to be gone for a while. Jackie's going to be riding you, so do your best. I promise I'll be back as soon as I can."

He breaks my hold and resumes frisking me for treats; satisfied that he's cleaned me out, he turns away and goes back to work on his hay. *Poor baby,* I think. *He doesn't know what it means to have me be away.* I want to weep at his innocence. *Is this normal?* I wonder. I look around, but there's no one to ask.

I'm three days into the trip before I manage to catch Jackie out of the saddle. "He misses you terribly," she says. She then proceeds to tell me that she's just taught Eli how to half-pass, a third-level lateral movement that requires more balance, engagement, and collection than my training-level horse could possibly have. Knowing Jackie as I do, however, I have no doubt Eli is indeed half-passing and doing it brilliantly.

"That's great," I say weakly, wondering what she'll have him doing by the time I get home. Making her dinner? Driving her truck?

Fortunately, she comes to her senses. I return to an exhausted Eli and a trainer as contrite as Jackie gets, which is not very. "I have to watch myself with him," she says. "He's so willing, I find myself teaching him things he's not physically ready for."

Because I have no such problems, I simply nod and keep my mouth shut, though I am reassured to hear her acknowledge his limitations.

My relief is short-lived. A few days later, as she's working on Eli's nonexistent trot-canter transition, I see her put both reins in her left hand, the better to whack him harder with the dressage whip in her right. Recalling the unfortunate muck rake incident, I wince at the sound, but I bite my tongue rather than question her methods.

Twenty minutes later, his sides coated with sweat, I relocate my backbone and suggest we leave it for another day. "No. We are going to get through this *today,*" she says in a tone that leaves no room for any further meddling. I understand her reasoning; you always want to end a training session on a positive note, because horses tend to remember the last thing they were taught.

But that's also why it rarely pays to push them in a new direction toward the end of a session, lest it drag on beyond the hour most trainers consider a reasonable amount of time for a young horse to work.

When, after nearly ninety minutes, I finally lead my wretched horse to the wash stall for a much-needed shower, he looks at me as if to say, *"Where the hell were you when I needed you?"* I feel awful for failing to protect and rescue him, and vow then and there never to let it happen again.

Instead, it happens again. And again. And again. I commiserate with Susan over coffee at the diner. "What the hell is *wrong* with me? Why am I such a wuss?"

"It's not just you," she says, "it's everyone. Nobody talks back to Jackie."

That may be true, but it's of little consolation when I'm sitting there silently, seemingly complicit, as she whacks Eli yet again with her whip.

Meanwhile, in barns the world over, the debate rages on as to the most effective way to discipline horses for behavior ranging from mildly unacceptable to downright dangerous. At one end of the spectrum are the people who believe that physical punishment is the only correction a horse understands. At the opposite end are the folks who feel that walloping an animal is never justified. As one might expect, there's a vast middle ground occupied by those who maintain that on the rare occasions when it's warranted, one quick smack on the rump or the shoulder— and no more than one—within a second or two of the offending behavior can go a long way toward preventing a recurrence.

The middle ground strikes me as the most reasonable of the three, though it's probably worth noting that despite considerable heated discussion, no one seems to be changing anyone's mind.

A week later, I surprise all three of us by spontaneously growing a pair and informing Jackie at the end of a lesson that for the time being, anyway, my horse and I have had quite enough. "I'm taking him back for a while," I say, hoping the quaver in my voice isn't audible across the arena. "I really think he could do with a break."

Then Jackie surprises me right back. "Good idea. Let him get his confidence back."

We hit the trails with Karen and her Thoroughbred, and even with her constant reminders for me to ease up on the reins, relax my seat, and *chill the hell out already,* I almost manage to enjoy myself. This, despite Eli's penchant for spooking at each and every sewer drain we pass, along with the air brakes on every delivery truck and the occasional chained, barking dog.

Is it my imagination, or is he doubly affectionate during our three-week vacation from training? Either way, I'm clearly not imagining the cold shoulder I'm getting from Jackie and her inner circle, an ever-changing cast made up of whichever boarders happen to be taking lots of lessons and riding particularly well at any particular time.

It's a fact of life that people hit horses. They hit them with crops, whips, or the flat of their hands. They hit them with whatever's within reach. They hit them because horses are very big, very strong animals in need of even stronger leaders, the kind who aren't afraid to correct them.

But the form that the correction takes—along with the timing and the degree—can make all the difference between building a relationship based on fear and one based on trust. In most situations, hitting a horse is only one way to make a point. In most situations, there are better ways.

Jackie has already told me I'm "too nice," and that my niceness will ultimately detract from my riding by precluding me from Getting the Job Done, whether by digging my spurs into Eli's sides, giving him a good, swift kick, an emphatic tap with the whip, or all three. Love isn't enough; horses need discipline.

I find myself pondering limits. Who should set them? And what should they be? And as long as I'm at it, what does love mean to a horse, anyway? How, if at all, does a horse experience love? And how does respect factor into the equation?

Back on Hickory Lane, I witness the moms grappling with much the same thing as they struggle to home in on the proper blend of discipline, indulgence, and love. Like me with my horse, they find themselves tested at every turn. If one cookie is good, two are better. If two are okay, why not four?

It seems obvious to me where they should be drawing the line, but then again, these aren't my children. Hence the clarity—and with it comes a new observation: When one is being tested, there's a lot to be said for outweighing the tester.

Body language being the native tongue, so to speak, of the horse, I watch Eli's movements for silent signs of contentment or displeasure: the lowering of his head, the softening of his eye, the lifting of a hind leg in warning. I listen, too, for his vocalizations: his nickered greetings; the short, sharp exhale, or "blow," signifying excitement; the whinnies telegraphing distress.

I also monitor the tilt and angle of his ears for signs of happiness, relaxation, attention, anger, anxiety, or fear. With sixteen muscles controlling their movement, those swiveling ears can speak volumes to anyone who's learned to crack their code.

Of course, I only have so many hours a week in which to do all this. Eli doesn't live with me, after all. And that's a good thing in some ways, for it frees me from the twice-daily feedings, the mucking out of his stall, the relentless chores that go along with horse ownership.

But it also begs another round of questions: Does he miss me? Does he think of me when I'm not around? The sight of his face in the window watching for my car seems to indicate that he does. Then again, how do I know that it's me he is watching for, when he could just as easily be watching the grass grow or the sun rise?

The blank slate onto which I project my not inconsiderable insecurities begins to assume the shape of a 16.2 Thoroughbred. Would Eli be happier with a stronger or better rider? Would he be progressing more rapidly? Am I holding him back?

From there, it's just a hop, skip, and a jump to an even deeper worry: Is it an ordeal for him to have me on his back? Does he hate having to haul my ass around?

Once I start down this slippery slope, I might as well be on a runaway bobsled. And though I do realize these are projections of my own insecurities as opposed to some deep, hidden thoughts on the part of my horse, that doesn't stop me from having them. Not for a single minute.

As always, Missy and Susan help chase away my mis-givings. "You treat him like gold," Susan says. "He couldn't possibly be any happier."

There are times—though not enough of them to suit me—when even I would be hard-pressed to argue, times when some mysterious synapse in his unknowable brain sud-denly fires, releasing a magical burst of what appears to be love and affection. At such times he greets me like a long-lost friend, nickering softly, staring deep into my eyes, snuf-fling the front of my T-shirt or burrowing his nose under my hair, the better to blow his sweet grassy breath on my neck.

I have no way of knowing what triggers these gestures; nor is it possible for me to know what miraculous impulse inspires him early one morning to gently take my cheek in his rubbery lips in what is obviously an uncanny imita-tion of the way I kiss him.

Of course, once he discovers that this ingenious ma-neuver is a surefire guarantee of a treat, there's no stopping him. Not that I would, of course. I'm only too happy to let him kiss me all day, though I do learn to keep a clean towel handy for mop-ups.

I'm well aware of the disapproving looks I get from more experienced horse owners when I treat Eli less like livestock than a beloved companion, less like an animal than a four-legged child.

Although I'm undoubtedly guilty of countless crimes against nature, also known as horse-handling sins, I consider them venial, not cardinal. Permitting Eli to rest his head on my shoulder. Allowing him to brush my cheek with his lips. Letting him rub my back with his muzzle. All are big no-no's, strictly speaking, among the barnyard Gestapo.

For the record, I am familiar with the rules I am breaking. Even though I'm allowed to move in and out of Eli's personal space, I shouldn't let him violate mine. Nor should I let him nose around in my pockets for treats. Such actions undermine my authority and have the potential to lead him to the unfortunate conclusion that he outranks me as a member of the herd. These and other pet-like behaviors are precisely the sort that can come back to bite an inexperienced horse owner like me.

I'm not fool enough to deny that he's spoiled. But so is my husband. So is my dog. Why should my horse be any different, aside from the fact that he *is* a horse?

I also realize I wouldn't be getting away with all this spoiling if Eli wasn't such a sweet, even-tempered creature. Most of the time, anyway.

I confess that I have also caught glimpses of Eli's darker side, on days when all it takes to turn his world upside down is a tube of worming paste or a soapy sponge aimed at his face. And though I've seen no evidence of meanness whatsoever in my horse, my darling does have a bit of a temper.

An angry Thoroughbred is a sight to behold, with his pinned ears and thrusting head, stamping his expensively shod hoof on the barn's concrete floor hard enough to throw a shower of sparks.

A 1,200-pound animal in the throes of a temper tantrum obviously is no joke, yet there are times when I find myself biting my lip and turning away to disguise my amusement. He is so like a gigantic toddler, compliant one minute, out of control the next, his oversized moods seeming to turn on a dime.

So, too, his taste buds. The current list of unacceptable treats is already as long as his face and includes any number of items that horses supposedly cannot resist, from apples—all varieties except the occasional Granny Smith—to molasses cookies, any kind other than "his" brand.

Even carrots, his favorite, occasionally fail to meet his impeccable standards. Once he's rejected a treat, for whatever reason, his suspicions are primed, and the next several offerings are subjected to rigorous product testing, which they invariably fail.

"Would you look at this," I say to Jackie, as my horse elaborately sniffs a peppermint candy the size of a quarter for fully half a minute before refusing to put it in his mouth. "He acts like I'm trying to poison him."

Jackie gives me a what-else-is-new shrug. "It comes with the territory. He *is* a Thoroughbred."

He is. And this summation is one I will hear again and again, a conversation ender that will be applied to a wide range of equine behaviors from skittishness to full-blown Looney Tunes. And though it's the nature of all horses to run away first and ask questions later, none runs so fast or so far as a Thoroughbred when confronted by the unexpected. Damn near everything, to a Thoroughbred, is unexpected.

Even though Eli is clearly cut from this same cloth, more experienced horse owners than I seem to agree that he's significantly more sensible than most. And though I have no basis for comparison, over time I will compile an impressive array of evidence bearing them out.

Fortunately, Eli's default mode is neither anger nor skittishness but playfulness, as evidenced by his habits of stealing the hose when I'm cooling him down, or tugging on my sleeve and then looking away, feigning innocence. He's also developed a begging routine subject to last-minute derailment should I fail to be charmed: his pawing right front leg—horse-speak for *"Hand over the cookies and no one gets hurt"*—transitions into an elaborate stretch accompanied by a big, phony yawn.

Turned loose when he's feeling good, he squeals like a pig, a high-pitched *"Whee!"* that's two parts excitement, one part "watch out"—good advice, since more often than not, it's closely followed by a series of bucks. He loves to roll on his back, then pop up and rear up before taking off running full-tilt. If I fail to play along, he usually eggs me on by running up to within inches of me and shaking his head in my face, violating my personal space once again.

It's when I'm sad or upset, though, that he truly displays the inherent sensitivity of his breed, as I discover one spring afternoon during our first year together. I'm en route to the barn for a lesson with Jackie when another driver pulls out into traffic and hits my car broadside. She then proceeds to scream at *me* for having gotten in her way. She threatens to leave the scene while I wait for a cop; when he finally comes, she gives him a fictional account of how the accident occurred. Fortunately, a witness steps up.

Although my car is still drivable, I'm more than an hour late by the time I get to Oakwood. I'm also in tears. I pull Eli out of his stall just as Jackie emerges from the indoor. I start telling her what happened. Having ascertained that I'm only shook up as opposed to hurt, though, she stops me midway.

"Look at Eli," she says, so I do.

Having planted himself in my path and lowered his head so we're eyeball to eyeball, he is gently and rhythmically bumping his nose against the front of my sweater.

"He sees you're upset," Jackie says, "and he wants it to stop."

I marvel at his complexity, his vast repertoire of moods, sometimes displayed within a single, exhausting day: playful, affectionate, demanding, obstreperous, mischievous, pensive, needy, excited, rambunctious, petulant, lazy, frightened, fresh, and forlorn.

More than anything, I love watching Eli show off, tail held high, nostrils flared, trotting with his legs so extended he seems to be floating on air between strides. No matter how many times I watch him do this, it never fails to quicken my heart.

The more I get to know him, the more aspects he displays of a personality that continues to evolve. But even I am amazed by his show of conscience the morning I arrive to find him glued to his window, clearly agitated and completely uninterested in both the carrot and the bucket of grain in my hands.

"What is it?" I ask as I finally unlatch his door and skirt a pile of manure to stand beside him and see what he sees: The dark shadow of a loose horse, moseying about the grounds. "Good boy!"

I grab a halter and throw a handful of sweet feed into a pail, then go outside to round up the runaway. Only then, when I have the wanderer securely in hand, do I see the shadow of Eli's head dipping in and out of his feed bucket as he tucks into the breakfast he has now more than earned.

seven

FALL 1997

ITH JACKIE PLANNING TO HEAD TO FLORIDA on the first day of the new year, January 1, 1998, for three months to train her own horses, I look forward to my second winter with Eli like a teenager whose parents are about to leave town. Much as I admire and value Jackie as a trainer, I'm beginning to chafe at what feels to me more and more like oversupervision.

Her rules seem to be multiplying, and I seem to be landing in the doghouse with some regularity for having broken them: for contacting the farrier directly instead of relaying my questions through her; for grabbing a muck rake and removing a pile of manure from Eli's otherwise pristine stall. Rather than commend me for my initiative, Jackie tells me not to do it again lest *everyone* start cleaning their horses' stalls.

She looks askance at the apple-green polo wraps I buy to protect Eli's legs, and lets it be known she'd prefer I buy white ones.

Even worse than her rules is her spy network, whose surveillance will soon land me in deeper trouble.

Although I'm not altogether sorry she's going away, there's also a downside: cooler weather has arrived, and after a long, hot summer that mellowed him out rather nicely, under saddle Eli is once again full of beans, throwing his head around, pulling the reins out of my hands, stamping his feet, and spooking over nothing at all. His energy is manageable as long as I have Jackie around to wear him out, but I'm already worried about how I'll cope once winter arrives and she's gone. I suspect I'll have my hands full.

By the time Thanksgiving rolls around, I'm still trying to figure out how to deal with this. When Karen, Eli's first rider and champion, suggests I turn him loose in the indoor to get his ya-yas out, I'm only too happy to take her advice. A little buck-fest followed by some running around— difficult for him to pull off in his steep, rocky paddock— could be just the ticket to keeping him manageable under tack. Not knowing—but suspecting—how Jackie would feel about this, I suggest we try it under cover of darkness.

Early the next morning, Karen and I lead Eli into the indoor arena, slide the doors closed behind us, and unfasten his lead rope. For an instant, he stands perfectly still, looking at us. He then pops his head up and sniffs the air, a gesture that over time I will come to associate with being in imminent danger of all hell breaking loose.

This time, however, I am completely unprepared for what happens next: Eli rears up on his hind legs like a *Tyran-*

nosaurus rex. And then, with a cloud of dust, he proceeds to treat us to a dazzling display of speed unlike anything I've witnessed this side of a racetrack.

It just so happens my baby can *run.* Unfortunately, he can also stop short inches away from the back wall, with a little leap to one side that can't possibly be good for him.

I look over at Karen, who's frowning. "Don't let him do that again."

"Fine," I say. "How do I stop him?"

She grabs a lunge whip and tosses another at me. "Go run down to the far end and wave him on as he goes by," she says.

By the time he's done running laps and is ready to be recaptured, he's also much too hot for me to saddle. In addition, he's blowing like a bellows, with veins bulging out all over his neck. Rather than ride him, I hand-walk him for what seems like hours, waiting for his breathing to return to normal.

I must say I am more than a little impressed by this amazing display of raw horsepower. I only wish I'd brought a video camera.

The air is too cold for me to hose him off, so I walk him back into the barn, grab a towel, and rub his sweaty coat till it's dry. I brush him all over, pick the dirt from his hooves, and throw his lightweight sheet on to protect him from the chill. I then drive home in a rosy glow that lasts right through till the following morning, when he hobbles out of his stall on three legs.

I'm in the wash stall running cold water over his swollen right front leg and beating myself up for having let this happen to him when Jackie arrives and sticks her regal red head in.

"Don't chase him around with a lunge whip," is all she says, but it's enough—*more* than enough—to make me feel doubly ashamed and extremely annoyed with whichever one of her spies tipped her off. Even money says it's Jesse. When the barn manager flounces by without giving us a second look, I have all the confirmation I need.

This time, at least I know how to poultice and wrap him. I also know from the heat and swelling in his lower right leg that he's probably strained a ligament. I'll be lucky if that's all he did.

For the next several weeks, I continue to hose and wrap, poultice and hand-walk my horse for twenty to thirty minutes at a time, an exercise that becomes progressively more difficult and dangerous by the day. Even though Jackie is still my trainer, I'm reluctant to go to her for advice. I did, after all, bring this on myself by letting Eli run around. Call me stubborn. But my horse is my responsibility; his behavior, my problem.

The better he feels, the bigger the ordeal. We set off at a brisk pace, a chain over his nose to keep him respectful and a crop in my hand to keep his hooves off my feet. Ten or fifteen minutes in, the entertainment begins.

He starts by lagging behind, alternately stamping his feet and shaking his head, or worse, rearing up on his hind legs. I feel like a third-rate lion tamer in a second-rate circus. I also wish I'd paid closer attention to those horse-handling rules.

Karen, who's in the ring with us, perfectly poised as usual as she rides her perfectly behaved horse perfectly, suggests that I pick up the pace. So I do, though I'm practically gasping for breath as it is. By the time we're done, Eli isn't the only one who's broken a sweat.

If he's this full of it, I can only assume he's feeling better. After a month of this regimen, I jog him in hand for the vet, who agrees.

Shortly before her scheduled New Year's Day departure, Jackie asks Karen to work with us while she's away, a plan we're all happy with. With Eli mended, we take a last lesson with Jackie, which Karen observes to get a sense of what stage of training we've reached. Jackie will monitor our progress long-distance and will make one or two weekend visits home to teach us along with her other students.

"One thing, though," Jackie says. "I don't want you cantering him till I'm back."

With her help, I've only just started working on Eli's canter. His stride is huge, and his transitions are rocky, so I'm not about to butt heads with her over this.

Our lessons with Karen are productive and fun, and even though she's nowhere near the powerhouse that Jackie is, she's an elegant and talented rider with a light touch that Eli seems to appreciate.

In addition to our time in the ring, we spend hours on the phone discussing the finer points of dressage and dissecting the strengths and weaknesses of the various horses and riders we know. I like having another new horse-loving friend, someone I can talk to about all things equine, including my occasional bouts of riding-related performance anxiety, a topic I never felt comfortable sharing with Jackie the Fearless.

One morning, after having finished riding and cooling out my horse, I lead him back into his stall. With one last carrot and a final pat on his muscular neck, I turn to head out. That's when I hear it, a cross between a grunt and a belch, a horrid, guttural, unmistakably heart-sinking sound emanating from my horse's stall, a sound that can only mean one very bad thing.

I flash back to one of my earliest days at the barn, watching Jackie fasten a thick leather strap that circles her horse's head from forehead to throat. "What on earth is that?" I ask.

"It's a cribbing strap. He's a cribber."

"What's a cribber?"

"A horse that grabs hold of something solid, like his stall door, arches his neck and sucks in air," Jackie says.

"Why, in God's name?"

"It supposedly releases endorphins that horses can get a mild high from," she says matter-of-factly, giving the strap a final tightening tug.

"Huh," I say, thinking, *Boy, does THAT ever look stupid. I'd hate to have a horse that has to wear one of THOSE.*

Now that I have one, much to my chagrin, I go home to read up on the subject. What I learn does not make me happy. According to animal behaviorists, cribbing is a re-action to the lifestyle we have foisted upon horses in the modern age. Confinement in solitary stalls and a diet of highly concentrated grain doled out two or three times a day does not a well-adjusted horse make. It's certainly a far cry from what nature intended, horses living in herds and free-ranging for food.

The consequences of this distorted way of life show up as anxiety, boredom, and stress. Some horses develop stom-ach ulcers. Some gnaw holes in their stalls. Others kick out at the walls and swing their heads from side to side in the repetitive motion known as weaving. Bored, unhappy horses wear paths in the floor boards from endlessly circling their stalls. Others paw, bite their own flanks, or crib.

The fact that cribbing is common makes it no less distressing; I now have proof that I've failed to provide adequately for my horse's needs. And as a result, he is filling his time with a harmful habit that's next to impossible to break. Now I know how parents of teenage smokers must feel.

The jury is still out on just how harmful a habit cribbing is. There's conflicting evidence on whether it makes horses more prone to colic, though it definitely causes unnatural wear to their teeth. There's no questioning the damage it does to fence rails, stall doors, even trees.

Cribbing straps, which put pressure on the larynx when the horse tries to arch his neck to suck in air, may deter the casual cribber, but for the hard-core addict, there's no easy solution, no Cribbers Anonymous, no rehab, not yet.

Nonetheless, I invest in the strap, along with an assortment of expensive stall toys: a rotating apple-scented rubber thingy that mounts in a corner and is supposed to be a real blast; a scented ball with a handle Eli can use to pick it up with his mouth, God only knows to what end; and solid treat balls that resemble bird seed and that hang by a rope from the ceiling, promising "no more bored horses!"

"*There*," I say to Eli, giving his treat ball a little test twirl. "Isn't *this* going to be fun? It's like *Disneyland* in here! I'll bet you're having trouble deciding what to play with first! Am I right?"

He looks at me blankly, then sets his teeth on his feed bucket, arches his neck, and sucks air, letting out a resounding belch. And so it goes till I've tried every toy I can find, all of which Eli ignores in favor of his endorphin addiction. The cribbing strap slows him down not one whit. If anything, the problem seems to be getting worse, with him at it again the minute I turn my back to leave.

Watching him, I have no doubt that he's cribbing for all the reasons the experts give for why horses crib: the boredom, the isolation, the empty hours between meals. Thinking of him thus—purposeless and idle, anxious and alone—drives me nuts. I can all but hear the mournful sound of a prison harmonica in my head: *"Nobody knows the trouble I've seen . . ."*

But having also seen Eli standing impatiently by the gate in his paddock on days when he desperately wants to come in—when the sun is brutally hot or the flies particularly bad—it's hard for me to believe he'd prefer to live outside 24/7. And though paddocks are a far cry from wide open spaces, a horse can get every bit as bored outside as in.

The social aspect, though, his need and desire to be with others of his species and my inability to be comfortable with that, fills me with guilt and remorse. I can well imagine how much Eli would love to have a playmate, another gelding to romp with in his paddock. As much as I hate to deny him the company of other horses, I'm stymied by his failure to respond to their body language in a way that makes any sense at all, or, failing that, a way that at least keeps him from getting hurt.

The kick that he suffered as a yearling, the one responsible for the smile-shaped scar just below his right knee, appears to have taught him nothing. Were he to be turned out with another horse, I don't doubt for a minute he'd leave himself open to more of the same. Judging from the old scar, it was a miracle he hadn't been injured more seriously. Next time he might not be so lucky.

I first witness his lack of acuity one morning as we're making our way back down the aisle from the wash stall. Eli suddenly stops dead in front of a stall occupied by a relative newcomer, a bay mare. He lifts his head, his eyes bright, his ears pricked forward in genial greeting. She takes one look at his hopeful, handsome, freshly shampooed chestnut face, lays her ears back and shows him her teeth.

He seems to think this must mean that she really, really likes him. Only after she kicks her stall door and lunges at him with her mouth open does he reluctantly allow me to drag him away, a scene that will be replayed with more horses more times than I care to count. As a result, I am forced to conclude that putting him out with another horse could be dangerous for him.

Hard as that is, there is nothing more painful than watching someone you love fall head over hooves for someone who does not love him back. When Eli falls, he falls hard, and not for superficial qualities like youth or beauty. No, when my gelding loses his heart, he invariably loses it to ancient blind ponies; fat, elderly mares; and swaybacked bags of bones.

And though I'd like to think these are largely affairs of the mind, there's no mistaking his ardor when Eli goes a-courting, prancing back and forth in his paddock with his reproductive equipment on display for all to see, professing his love and devotion with a series of whinnies so loud and so shrill, one can't help but be moved as well as deafened.

Ah, me. My baby is truly a fool for love.

₊

THAT GELDINGS SOMETIMES act like stallions isn't exactly a news flash, but love? Bandying that word about in most barns will get you slapped with a charge of anthropomorphism in the first degree.

Whoa there a minute. Back up. Not so fast.

Although humans have long been believed to have cornered the market when it comes to emotion, animal behaviorists are using advanced tools such as PET (positron emission tomography) scans to prove otherwise. PET scans that record brain activity and chemical changes in response to specific stimuli are letting scientists evaluate the mental state of horses that are responding to the deaths of close companions within their herds.

Along with behaviors that mimic those of grieving humans—loss of appetite and weight, withdrawal from social activity, a weakened immune system, and so on—the mourning horses' PET scans show patterns closely corresponding to those of people suffering from clinical depression. Having seen horses exhibit such behaviors in response to the loss of a friend, I'm not the least bit surprised.

As Sharon Crowell-Davis, DVM, PhD, a board-certified animal behaviorist at the University of Georgia, told the *Thoroughbred Times,* "When animals are recorded showing the same patterns of brain activity and the same brain chemical changes that correspond to a particular human emotion or mood state, it would not be logical for us to assume that they are not experiencing similar feelings."

Indeed. Although I don't doubt that horses do, in fact, feel the full gamut of painful human emotions, the insight weighs on me. The prospect of watching Eli grieve absent the knowledge that this, too, shall pass seals the deal as far as a pasture mate is concerned. There's no way I can let him be turned out with a friend, especially one that is just passing through.

* ★ *

AS THE WEEKS GO BY, Karen, Eli, and I continue to make slow, steady progress toward our goal of impressing Jackie, who's due back for two days of lessons in late February. On the eve of her return, Karen puts Eli and me through one last workout and we jointly pronounce him ready to dazzle.

Tacking him up for Jackie the following afternoon, I flash back to the first time I readied him for her, marveling at how far we have come. "Don't you worry," I whisper into his chestnut ear. "This time you're ready. And you're going to do great."

And he does. For twenty minutes, through countless changes of direction and gait, Jackie rides Eli without a single correction as Karen and I look on like proud parents. When she finally brings him to a halt directly in front of us, it's all I can do to keep from throwing my arms around him.

Then: "He feels awful," she says flatly.

I feel punched in the stomach. "What are you *talking* about?"

Rather than answer me, Jackie peels off her jacket and proceeds to work the crap out of him while Karen and I look on, stricken. After Jackie has wordlessly handed me the reins to my sweaty, exhausted gelding, I lead him back into the barn to cool him down and fume.

"How bad could he be?" I hiss at Karen. "She didn't correct him once."

"I know," Karen says.

"Maybe she's ridden too many upper-level horses. Maybe she's forgotten what a green horse ought to feel like."

Whatever the issue, it doesn't bode well for my lesson the following day. Sure enough, I'm a wreck before I even get on him, anxious, tense, and stiff as a board. We're still warming up in the indoor when a minor avalanche of ice and snow suddenly lets go and cascades off the tin roof directly over our heads, sounding like the end of the world.

Eli does his usual 180 and makes a run for it, as I pitch forward and try to hold on, only vaguely aware of Jackie bellowing at me to "SIT BACK!" When I finally do, Eli stops running and settles into a Thoroughbred jig. "You are *never* going to get *anywhere* till you learn to *sit back*," Jackie says in a tone of utter resignation and disgust; all this in front of a sizable audience of boarders.

There's no recovering my poise after that. We limp through our lesson on jangly nerves, Jackie yelling, Eli prancing, me cringing. Even though I know what to do, I can't seem to do it; I can't make my body relax and respond the way I want it to, and therefore, for the life of me, I can't do anything right.

When it's finally over, I lead Eli back to the barn, where I remove his tack and avoid eye contact with the other boarders, then berate myself all the way home. Later, I debrief in an hourlong phone call with Karen, who apologizes for having walked out in a fury without so much as a word to me.

I feel betrayed yet again by my defective body. I feel like a malfunctioning mess.

Over dinner that night, my husband takes it all in: my reddened eyes, my humiliation, my fury, my misery, and asks the question any reasonable human being might very well ask: "Why are you doing this to yourself? Why not just ride your horse and enjoy him?"

And I respond as any miserable, humiliated, infuriated human being very well might: condescendingly. "You don't understand. This is how dressage *is*. I don't want to 'just ride my horse,' I want to ride him *correctly*."

He raises an eyebrow but knows enough not to say another word. We finish our dinner in silence.

The next morning, I slink into the barn and follow a very loud, very rhythmic, very guttural sound down the aisle to my horse's stall. There I find Eli out cold in a heap on his shavings, snoring away like an asthmatic grampa after Thanksgiving dinner.

I'm in the tack room waiting for him to regain consciousness when Jackie sweeps in to gather her belongings for her return trip to Florida. We give each other a subdued greeting, whereupon I busy myself with rearranging my trunk. I have no real desire to revisit the past couple of days, especially not now, not with her. But she pauses on her way out and says not unkindly, "I think it would help you to keep Eli tired."

* ⋆ *

I KNOW WHAT *WON'T* HELP ME: dwelling on the debacles of the weekend. Unfortunately, I can think of little else. My self-confidence in the saddle, never anything much to write home about in the first place, has taken a very big, very public hit, and I have no idea how to regain it.

Also, paranoid as it sounds, I can't help but feel as though Jackie did it on purpose, adding a layer of betrayal to my embarrassment and shame. Instead of helping me regain my composure, she scolded me for having lost it. I, in turn, responded to her scolding by becoming more flustered than I already was. I then transmitted all that tension right back to my horse, a perfect negative feedback loop.

In the context of my athletic prowess (or the lack thereof) I'm back on old, familiar ground: my grammar school playground, where I was perhaps the only student in the history of Bluff School who was unable to traverse the monkey bars; the softball field at summer camp, where I struck out every time I went up to bat; eighth-grade gym class, where my technique on the trampoline was used as an object lesson in what *not* to do.

It's familiar ground, all right. And it's strewn with land mines.

On my forty-five-minute drive to and from the barn, I treat myself to a tour of these and other low points of four decades of participation in sports, four decades that rarely proved to be anything but degrading.

I blame polio, the mild bout at age three that impelled me to stop walking and resume crawling. The partial paralysis only lasted a few weeks, but I still remember the frustration of being offered treats that I desperately wanted but could only have if I managed to walk to them.

Unlike so many of the tens of thousands of victims of the polio epidemic of the 1950s, I was lucky. Physically, polio left me with a very slight limp that only became noticeable when I was tired. But emotionally, it also left me with something else: a shameful secret. Something was wrong with me; I had some kind of defect. And I lived in fear of anyone finding out.

I managed to keep my impairment to myself for seven years before it was finally brought to light—not by a doctor, but by the owner of a local shoe store who'd noticed an unusual wear pattern on the bottom of my left Stride Rite. Visits to hospitals ensued. At one, I had to strip down to my underpants and run up and down the halls while a team of male orthopedic specialists scrutinized my flawed gait and debated the merits of fixing it.

Local doctors wanted to operate; the specialists at Boston Children's Hospital pronounced it too late. They sent me home with my defect, a prescription for orthopedic shoes, and a set of exercises to be done with me on my back on the dining room table, my father manipulating my legs.

I hated the shoes almost as much as I hated the exercises, a daily reminder that I was damaged goods. Horseback riding, the one physical activity I loved, might have repaired my self-image if not my limp. But my overprotective family became even more so. By the time kids my age were winning ribbons at shows, the only horses in my life were the ones I saw from the car window as we drove past the fields north of town.

Although technically a city, Claremont, New Hampshire, population 12,000, was in all the important ways a small town. It was also a company town, a mill town, a Catholic town. Fathers worked for Joy Mining Machinery, by far the biggest employer. Mothers, for the most part, stayed home.

We were different. Not "good" different. Just different. Trust me: there's a difference.

We were Jewish, for one thing, and our walking route to the modest synagogue on High Holy days took us right past our schools, invariably during recess. Classmates paused their playing to gawk at us as we paraded by in our good clothes. Our teachers were nothing if not unenlightened. During the month of December, while our classmates sang carols, the teachers invited me and my best friend, Martha, the only other Jewish kid in my grade, to wait out in the hall. It was there that my lifelong obsession with ornaments, tinsel, and the other trappings of the forbidden holiday was born.

We were different in other ways, too. We owned a store, Shulins Inc., the retail side of the family business, which sold fabrics, draperies, bedspreads, and notions; *schmattes,* in the Yiddish of my grandparents. Situated in the center of town with our name emblazoned on the marquis, the store was open six days a week, letting anyone who felt like it walk in and encounter one or more of my relatives doing something cringe-worthy, like breathing.

Unlike mine, the vast majority of the other kids' parents and grandparents were not on public display but were tastefully hidden away in their homes or in the mills, allowing their offspring to pretend they'd been hatched from anonymous eggs, the fond dream of self-conscious adolescents everywhere.

I had no such luck. "I saw your grandmother," someone would announce in an accusatory tone in a junior high school cafeteria turned suddenly silent. I'd toss off a witty retort—"Bully for you" was a favorite—and pray for the ground to open and swallow me whole.

Things only got worse after my sister and I were pressed into modeling a new line of ponchos for the store. Despite makeovers, we looked nothing like models in the ad that appeared in the *Claremont Daily Eagle,* but more like two morose, unattractive little girls sporting oversized blankets and middle-aged hair.

At a time in my life when all I wanted was to be just like everyone else, the poncho episode was akin to being stripped bare and made to sleep in the front window of Shulins Inc., in the scale-model bed that served as a bedspread display. I still have nightmares about waking up there in front of a sizable crowd, naked but for my orthopedic shoes.

In addition to the store, we owned a wholesale business, Shulins Woolen Co., which occupied a low-slung warehouse sandwiched between ancient textile mills. Airless in summer and freezing in winter, the Taj Mahal, as my father dubbed it, was a dank, dirty cavern that reeked of a century's worth of stale air, moldy cardboard, wet wool, and dead rodents, and featured a bathroom so horrifying my sister and I were afraid to set foot in it no matter how badly we needed to go, though our father's hilarious descriptions of it never failed to send us into convulsions.

Personal humiliation aside, the Claremont of the 1960s had a certain cachet. Ours was the "It" town, at least compared with the towns that surrounded it. As kids, we dispatched each with a single unflattering adjective: Newport was a "hick" town; Cornish, a "cow" town; Windsor, a "skanky" town; Unity, too small a town to warrant a label at all.

Claremont, on the other hand, had winning high school athletic teams, cool new marching band uniforms, a drive-in movie theater, and its very own ski area, lit for night skiing and with Beatles music piped outside. (Not that I was ever allowed to go skiing at night.) There was also a happening downtown to cruise, *the* place to see and be seen, preferably from behind the wheel of one's own car, in one's boyfriend's car, or, as a last resort, in any car without an adult inside.

Regardless, no amount of smug superiority could disguise the hefty layer of yokel that lurked beneath our pseudo-sophisticated veneer. Our middle school curriculum featured such academic benchmarks as square dancing and penmanship. Saturday was Polka Night at the local radio station, when the strains of "Roll Out the Barrel" would compete with the droning engines of stock cars at Claremont Speedway. Sunday supper, our one nod to international cuisine, was takeout pizza prepared by the revolving rogues gallery of *mafiosi* said to be hiding out at Tony's Pizzeria, Claremont being the last place disgruntled business associates would think to look.

In high school, we partied in a cow pasture, got buzzed on Boone's Farm Apple Wine, and went parking in the cemetery. My English teacher left his wife and kids to marry a sophomore. Take away the drive-in and the spiffy new band uniforms and Claremont was an awful lot like its neighbors—a hick town, a cow town, even a skanky town if you knew where to look—only bigger.

A few major fires took their toll on our happening shopping district, including one, sparked by a wiglet under a hairdryer at the beauty school, that destroyed an entire downtown block one April Fool's Day. A stately old inn was demolished and replaced by an aesthetically challenged minimall. One by one, the fashionable shops that had lured savvy customers from distant towns disappeared, replaced by junky thrift stores masquerading as antique shops.

Then came the unthinkable: our company town's company pulled the plug on its Claremont operations. We thought of it as the end of the world. In fact, it was just the beginning of our languorous slide into decrepitude. (For more on this, see Flint, Michigan; Scranton, Pennsylvania; Canton, Ohio; and so on.)

I took to lying about where I was from, though I rationalized that it wasn't really, technically, a lie: "I was born in Hanover. You know, where Dartmouth College is?" I would say, conjuring the more desirable image of privileged frat boys amid Georgian Colonials. I glossed over the part where we left the hospital the next day and returned home to Claremont, where I was stuck for the next seventeen years.

In keeping with my ambivalence, there was a part of me that took a perverse satisfaction in my hometown's decline. Damaged as I was, it seemed only fitting that I should hail from an equally flawed place.

Like most of my friends, I couldn't wait to graduate from high school and get the hell out of Dodge. At Northeastern University in Boston everyone seemed to have come from New Jersey, a foreign land I'd grown up making fun of. From the Brahmins of Bergen County to the Panchamas of Paterson, though, theirs was a caste system far more refined than any I'd known in Cow Hampshire.

That I'd go on to spend seven years of my life in Hoboken, that perennial punch line on the Hudson, transcends irony. That my first beat as a freelance reporter would turn out to be Claremont could only be the result of bad karma, the kind that undoubtedly comes of having lied about one's hometown.

⋆

WITH KAREN'S HELP, I manage to recover my lost confidence in just a few rides, including one in which I handle a series of spooks so rambunctious, even the impassive Jesse is impressed.

"Way to stick like glue, girl," she says, giving me a thumbs up as she passes us en route to the hayloft. I'm elated, even as I'm berating myself for caring about what she thinks.

Just as the cold weather begins to moderate, I arrive at the barn on a Saturday morning to find a nasty-looking bruise vaguely shaped like a horseshoe on Eli's right shoulder. "What's this?" I ask Jesse, who informs me that Eli got kicked by one of the mares while in turnout.

I look at her uncomprehendingly. This is precisely the reason Eli gets turned out alone. "I don't get it. How did she manage to kick him from two paddocks away?"

Jesse's cheeks immediately redden and I feel a knot beginning to form in my stomach. She mumbles something unintelligible and hurries off to the tack room to busy herself with some imaginary chore. I follow hot on her heels.

I close the tack room door and confront her. "You need to tell me what happened," I say.

Jesse looks down at the floor and sighs heavily. "Bella's been going out with him," she says.

I must not be hearing right. *"What did you say?"*

"I said he and Bella have been going out together."

"What?" I can feel my blood pressure soaring into the stroke danger zone. "You turned him out with another horse? Without my permission? Are you *kidding* me?"

Jesse shrugs and turns away. "Hey, I just work here."

A surge of anger passes through me, turning my backbone to steel. "Call her up."

Instead, Jesse just stands there.

"Call her *now*," I bellow.

Wordlessly, Jesse drops a quarter into the pay phone on the wall and dials Jackie's number in Florida. I'm praying she'll pick up, and she does.

Jesse stretches the cord and disappears around the corner to speak privately as I wait in the tack room with a matching three-piece set of clenched fists and clenched jaw. When she finally hands me the phone, I waste no time on pleasantries.

"You *do not* have my permission to turn Eli out with another horse. What on earth made you think you could do that?"

Jackie lets out a sigh, shorthand for boarders are a pain in the ass, and says "He was perfectly happy going out with her."

"Well, he's not happy now, and neither am I. From now on, he goes out alone."

Another sigh. "Put Jesse back on."

I hand Jesse the phone, and she once again disappears around the corner. When she reappears to hang up the phone, her cheeks are flushed scarlet and she walks by me without a word. I trail after her. "Jesse, stop. What did she say?"

Jesse looks at her boots. "She said keep doing it until something happens."

I feel murderous rage. "Get her back on the phone."

This time, I grab the receiver from Jesse before she has a chance to speak. "This ends *now*. Not 'when something happens.' Something already did. Unless you're planning to start paying my vet bills, Eli goes out alone. End of discussion."

"Let me talk to Jesse," is all she says.

I return to a nicker and a nuzzle from my bruised horse. "That does it," I tell him. "We're getting the hell out of here."

eight

1998

W E MOVE. TWICE. First, to a backyard barn with no indoor ring, which is fine for the summer. The new place has the added benefit of being less than a half-hour's drive from my house. It's also just a few miles from a quaint little eatery locally famous for its breakfasts, definitely a contributing factor in the number of friends who suddenly want to visit.

The new barn is snug and extremely well-built, a large repurposed garage with a window for Eli to hang his head out and a good-sized meadow adjacent to the property for us to ride in when we're tired of the ring.

The outdoor ring is a large, gently sloping affair with a dense row of bushes at the far end. They look perfectly harmless to me, but Eli begs to differ; he spooks at them regularly as we ride by. Although I could live without his skittishness, I do love having him close enough to be able to check on him in the evenings, to run over, feed him some carrots and tuck him in, so to speak, for the night.

At the same time, I miss Susan and Missy, along with all the other friends I'd made while we were at Oakwood. It's so much quieter here. I miss Jackie, too, though I can't say I miss Jesse. True to form, the barn manager responded to my giving notice by worrying about her own ass.

"That's ridiculous," I said when she voiced concern about taking the blame for our departure. "Jackie knows why I'm leaving. She could have fixed this easily enough. She chose not to. That tells me she doesn't really care."

Having said that out loud forces me to examine it. Why would Jackie have wanted us gone? I put the question to Susan the following weekend, over a diner breakfast destined to be our last for a while.

"She had to see this coming, right? I mean, what choice did I have? She was putting my horse in harm's way."

"I'm sure that wasn't her intent; she was just trying to appease a new boarder who wanted more turnout time for her horse. By putting the two out together . . ."

I finish it for her: "She could give the new boarder what she wanted. It just happened to be at Eli's expense."

"Right."

"I can't imagine her doing that to someone else's horse. What made her think she could do it to mine?"

"The fact that she found him for you," Susan says. "I'm sure she assumed she could go on calling the shots."

Looking at it from that perspective makes me feel better. It hadn't been anything personal.

In time, I would also come to understand her changed demeanor toward me as a reflection of the enormous pressure she put on herself as a result of her own advanced training. There's a reason most Grand Prix riders don't train novices.

Despite the circumstances under which I had left, I would always be grateful to Jackie for bringing me together with Eli.

This time, it was the right horse.

* ★ *

WITH WINTER FAST APPROACHING, Karen finds us an eighty-stall barn an hour's drive from my house. We arrange transport and arrive at Pegasus on a frigid January afternoon in the aftermath of an ice storm. As we inch our way toward the front door, I am grateful for the studs on Eli's shoes, the only things keeping us upright.

We walk in the front door to the sight of the biggest indoor arena I've ever set foot in. We meet the barn manager, a very young, very blonde, very shy woman named Erin, who shows us to Eli's new stall. I'm pleased to see that it's on an outside wall with another big window for him to hang his head out come spring, the boarding barn equivalent of big-screen TV.

I let Eli eat hay and settle in while I put our things away in the tack room. Mike, the affable barn owner, comes by to say hello. "This place is enormous," I say. "How will I ever find my horse again in here?"

He laughs. "It's a grid. The stalls are built around the indoor. All you have to do is keep walking and you'll end up right back where you started from."

Thus acclimated, I clip on a lead rope and invite Eli to come out and have a look around. He's on yellow alert, not quite ready to bolt, but hardly relaxed as we make our way down the roomy aisle between the stalls.

His wide eyes miss nothing: not the other horses, calmly eating their hay or resting quietly; not the Weimaraner napping outside the office; not the giant kerosene heater glowing red as it blows warm air into the enormous indoor; not the soda machine humming away in the corner.

All are unfamiliar sights and sounds, some more threatening than others. I steer clear of the dog and the heater for the moment, but otherwise, each time Eli pops his head up, plants his feet, and blows—*Danger! Proceed with caution!*—I talk to him softly and encourage him to walk up to the suspicious object and give it a sniff. In this manner, we slowly make our way around the grid.

I'm leading him around the indoor when I catch a glimpse of us in the mirrored side wall: Eli walking as close to me as I'm willing to safely allow, hanging back slightly, shyly peeking over my shoulder. I can't help but smile; his expression brings to mind an old photo of my nephew, his hair neatly combed, khakis pressed, and a blend of apprehension and excitement on his five-year-old face as he heads off on his first day of kindergarten.

If changing barns is hard on a horse, moving twice in a matter of months has to be doubly hard. I can only imagine how big and alien this place must seem to Eli after the summer in his little garage. But I can also sense his growing trust in me as together we explore this strange and stimulating new world.

I'm happy to see his ears swivel in my direction as I talk to him, relieved to see him occasionally blink. Out of nowhere, an aphorism pops into my head, something I once read or heard: When he's blinking, he's thinking;

when he's not, he's hot. If I'm able to keep or regain his attention without too much trouble, I'm reasonably confident he's not about to wig out.

I've only had him for a couple of years, and he's already lived in three barns and had two trainers. The only constant in his young life has been me. I hope that's enough to make him reasonably secure. I hope he's figured out by now that I'm his.

* * *

FOR THE NEXT WEEK OR SO, I show up before dawn to try to ease the transition for Eli. Fortunately, he seems to like the place. To me, it still feels enormous. But, like my horse, I soon acclimate. As always, our best time of day is early in the morning when it's quiet, except Pegasus is seldom quiet. One of the muckers apparently doubles as a mechanic. He always seems to be revving an engine out front.

Once he's done feeding horses, Mike likes to hold forth with his coffee, surveying his domain from just outside his office and chatting with whomever's around. More often than not, that means me.

We soon fall into an easy patter that largely consists of telling bad jokes badly, butting heads over politics, and trading barn gossip. But it isn't long after Eli and I arrive that I get to observe a more substantial side of him.

We're chatting as usual one morning when a young boarder asks him for help. She's trying to load her mare on a trailer bound for a medical procedure at a nearby clinic. It's been close to an hour, and she's having no luck. "Could you come out and see if you can get her on?"

"No problem," Mike says.

I follow him out to the parking area. The boarder's father is holding one end of a lead rope with the uncooperative mare at the other. I'd be hard-pressed to say which of them looks more frustrated.

"Why don't you go stand over there?" Mike says to the father, gesturing toward the cab of the truck to which the trailer is hitched. He takes the lead rope from the father and walks the mare in a big circle without coming anywhere near close to the ramp. He then changes direction and circles her the other way. The mare walks beside him without hesitation.

The first time he leads her toward the ramp, she stops short a few feet from it. He resumes circling her and tries again. Again she balks, and again he returns to the circle. She refuses again. And again.

Through it all, he shows no outward sign of frustration, his demeanor the same after seven refusals as it was when he first took the rope. On her next approach, the mare walks up the ramp and into the trailer, nice as you please. Mike fastens the butt chain behind her and closes the ramp, locking it in place. Greatly relieved, the father and daughter thank him profusely and head out.

"That was amazing," I tell him. "You really kept your cool."

"No reason to lose it," he says. "It doesn't do you any good."

With people, on the other hand, Mike tends to lose it with some regularity. His bellow can also be heard piercing the stillness at any time, since he lives on the premises in a trailer parked out back. The guy can *yell*. He isn't the type to suffer fools gladly. At the same time, though, his pa-

tience with Randy, his twenty-something mentally disabled helper, is limitless.

I learn that Randy's father pays Mike to pay Randy,
thereby affording him the dignity of having a job. The
horses, mine included, seem to "get" that he's disabled, and
though his movements can be jerky and abrupt, they
somehow understand that Randy can't help it and that he
means them no harm. They, too, are remarkably gentle
and patient with him. I never once see any of them so
much as pin their ears at him.

For Eli's first month at Pegasus, Karen and I make sure
he sees at least one of us every day. It helps—at least from
the standpoints of my schedule and my mental health—
that I've made a career change, having resigned from The
Associated Press after twenty-two years to write nonfiction
books, something I can do anywhere.

For the most part, I'd led a charmed life as one of a
handful of full-time feature writers at AP, an organization
best known for its global coverage of breaking news. Lately,
though, it had become increasingly apparent that my best
days at AP were behind me.

My editor, the animal lover I'd idolized for so long, had
been reassigned, resulting in a succession of regime
changes. I'd been under increasing pressure to work at the
New York office instead of my house in Connecticut, as I'd
been doing for years. With Eli an hour away in the opposite direction, I couldn't figure out how to make my life
work with a three-and-a-half-hour commute to the city
and back every day. As it was, if I didn't get up and go to
the barn at 4:00 or 5:00 AM, I'd undoubtedly not get there
at all.

In trying to balance my various commitments—husband, job, home, dog, and horse—I'd found myself wishing for a forty-hour day in order to shoehorn everything in. More and more, I'd been feeling like I was doing a fair-to-middling job at everything.

I was sad to be leaving so many old and close friends, but my department, sometimes referred to as "The Poet's Corner," was being dismantled, my colleagues encouraged to retire. An era, albeit a long, fruitful one, was ending. It was time to figure out my next act.

A twenty-four-hour diner with friendly waitresses just off the highway a couple of exits from the new barn becomes my de facto office, a place to sit and write while I wait for what passes for sun in the dead of January to come up.

I'm amazed at how quickly this barn goes from feeling enormous to feeling like home to both Eli and me. The more I get to know Mike, the better I like him. He's a friendly, no-nonsense horseman who exudes confidence, an expert wrangler whom the horses seem to trust intuitively.

I also like the mix of people and disciplines at this most highly democratic of barns, home to horses and people of all shapes and sizes, including a fair number of kids.

The affinity of young girls for horses is very much in evidence here, and after two adults-only boarding barns, it's nice to see children and ponies again. Watching a bevy of little girls fussing over even the homeliest of ponies, I'm reminded that beauty is in the starry eyes of the beholders. (However, the Twinkle® Toes Glitter Hoof Polish they're applying in Rodeo Pink can easily glam up the plainest pony. Fortunately, they've come fully supplied with a can of Ultra Instant Hoof Polish Remover.)

Glitter hoof polish had yet to be invented when I fell in love for the first time. Rhythm, an aged lesson horse, had to be thirty if he was a day, his once-white coat permanently stained with manure. But to me, he was the most beautiful creature in the United States of America, planet Earth, and the Milky Way galaxy.

Unfortunately, the day Rhythm dumped me on my head in the riding stable's driveway happened to be the same day I'd finally persuaded my jittery grandparents to come watch me ride. One minute I was proudly waving to them from high atop Rhythm's swayed back; the next, I was slowly regaining consciousness in the owner's bedroom, the ashen faces of my Nana and Gampie swimming into focus above me. Although I immediately forgave Rhythm his momentary lapse of good manners, I was the only one in my family who did.

Now, all these years later, I see my young self in these girls and I find myself envying them. There was a time, not that long ago, when I shared their uncritical gaze; when I, too, thought there was no such thing as an ugly horse. Now that I'm saddled with an educated eye, I know better. Even so, I still think every horse, beautiful or not, deserves at least one little girl who looks at him the way I looked at Rhythm. Or, as I'm becoming increasingly aware, the way a little girl named Greta looks at Eli.

The first time I see her, she's standing on tiptoe slipping treats through the bars on his stall door. I introduce myself, though she can't tear her eyes away from my horse long enough to meet me. I, on the other hand, do get to know Greta the Groupie quite well over time. She has a way of appearing from out of thin air wherever Eli happens to be.

For all its pervasiveness, the girlish infatuation with horses is no less mysterious to me at fifty than it was at seven or eight. I've always wondered why I had it and my sister did not; why she was content to play with her dolls (and mine) for hours on end, whereas I quickly tired of Barbie, abandoning her in favor of stick horses fashioned from broom handles, cheap plastic and ceramic horse figurines, and the ultimate fetish, the mechanical horse outside the five-and-dime.

I recall having plenty of girlfriends happy to share this childish horseplay with me, right up to and including horse camp, where we had the unspeakable luxury of being able to ride real live horses as often as three or four times a week.

Speed and strength, courage and beauty are but a few of the attributes for which horses have been exalted throughout history. But it is the horse as agent of transformation that most resonates with me when I look back on my five-year-old self. On the back of a horse, I was no longer small and powerless, no longer defective. That transformation must have been what I was seeking, whether I knew it or not, a kind of borrowed perfection I could try on for size, if only for an hour at a time.

That doesn't explain why my girlhood obsession, though dormant, survived in me for twenty-odd years, long after most of my horse-loving friends had moved on and left horses behind. In some, I detect a hint of wistfulness when they ask about Eli, but that seems to be as far as it goes.

Most are too busy being mothers to ride anymore, though a number of their daughters do. Had I succeeded in having children, I might not have found my way back to it, either. No question I wouldn't own Eli. But if I'd had a child who'd shown even a modicum of interest, I might very well be one of the moms I now see at barns satisfying their own equine cravings, if not by riding, then by lavishing attention on their children's horses.

Along with the pony lovers at Pegasus, I also see pint-sized barrel racers (also mostly female), middle-aged ropers (mostly male), and Western pleasure riders of both sexes. I see hunter-jumpers, draft horses, and the occasional dressage horse. It's a healthy blend of humans and disciplines after the competitive world of Jackie's dressage barn, and a timely reminder that it's okay just to have fun with my horse.

I can use the reminder after six months with Karen as my trainer. What began as an enjoyable, low-key trainer-student relationship is fast becoming a high-pressure, anxiety-filled nightmare. Karen seems intent on out-shouting Jackie. The more she screams at me to sit back, the more I curl up into a defensive ball, thereby prompting more screaming, a vicious cycle we're both only too happy to blame on me.

Caught in the middle, my poor horse absorbs all our tension until he explodes, whereupon the whole cycle starts anew.

I ask myself constantly why I'm allowing a trainer to ruin horse ownership for me, or, perhaps more to the point, why I'm ruining it for myself. What effect is all this tension having on Eli? Is it screwing him up? How can it not?

My internal debate rages on, leaving me emotionally depleted and—worse—alienated from my horse, without whom I wouldn't be in this untenable mess, defeated by my inability to follow my drill-sergeant's orders: SIT BACK! LEAN RIGHT! EYES UP! SHOULDERS BACK! STOP PERCHING!

SHORTEN YOUR REINS! LET! GO! OF! HIS! FACE! DROP YOUR REINS! DROP THEM! NOW! NOT TOMORROW!

By the time she gets around to yelling "YOU LOOK DE-FORMED," we are finally on the same page. This at least makes perfect sense; this I do understand. In my mind I *am* deformed, after all. It's only reasonable that I should look that way, too.

It's almost a relief when with a mixture of fury, frustration, and disgust she finally orders me off my horse and rides him herself, while treating me to a running commentary on everything I've screwed up that she now needs to fix.

Some days I look back on my first year with Jackie and wonder if Eli and I will ever make that kind of progress again, if I'll ever feel that heady blend of exhilaration and possibility, that growing competence that made riding so much fun. As it is, I am definitely backsliding, losing pieces of myself as I go.

And yet I keep training, my husband's and friends' questions echoing in my head: Why *can't* I just go on trail rides and enjoy my horse? Why *don't* I fire Karen and look for a more compassionate trainer? Because. Because I'm hooked on this impossible sport and its tantalizing glimpses of perfection.

Because I deserve to be yelled at. Because I have it coming. (My hands *are* bad. My position *is* wrong.)

Because there's something familiar about being belittled and beat up for my lack of athleticism.

Because I desperately want to learn how to do this.

Because I don't want to be coddled.

Because I'm not the only one Karen is doing this to.

Missy, my old friend from Oakwood, finally has a horse of her own. She, too, is boarding at Pegasus and training with Karen. And though she's a far more experienced rider than I, you wouldn't know it to eavesdrop on one of her lessons.

Bonnie, the strawberry blonde I met my first day at Oakwood, now keeps her horse here as well. She, too, has ridden much longer than I, yet her lessons leave her every bit as bedraggled, every bit as sweaty, exhausted, and red in the face. And in the rarefied world of dressage, this seems to be par for the course.

I know of several big-name dressage trainers in the area who are famously harsh with their students. I can only conclude that dressage and screaming trainers must go together, not unlike perfectionism and low self-esteem.

nine

MARCH 1999

*I*NVARIABLY, JUST WHEN I THINK I can't take another minute of Karen, Eli and I have a breakthrough. Everything she's been screaming about comes together in glorious fashion—proper use of my leg, seat, and hand, with Eli responding correctly—for the better part of a week, a day, an hour, even a moment or two.

On the rare occasions when this happens, all of the disparate bits and pieces I've been wrestling with become automatic. Riding becomes almost effortless. My body takes over and my big, stupid, meddlesome brain busies itself somewhere else. Eli and I are connected as if by some supple, invisible string. Hard becomes easy. Dressage becomes Zen.

Today has been just such a day. We've been riding serpentine loops—S-shaped patterns—at the canter, and we've done them well enough to impress. "Great job!"

Karen says. I treat Eli to an extra-long grazing session to celebrate, even though it's only mid-March and what little grass is out there is considerably more brown than green.

As bad as I feel about myself when I ride poorly, on the rare day like this, I am over the moon. I relish my soreness and replay our performance again and again on the movie screen in my head, impatient for tomorrow's lesson, breathlessly eager to build on today's success. On days like this, I pity every person who's never known the joy of doing a "great job" of riding a horse. I can think of nothing I'd rather be doing.

Endorphins are a beautiful thing.

I wake up the next morning even before my alarm, and dress in the bathroom so as not to wake Mark. He, too, has changed jobs, having left AP to work for an Internet publishing company a few miles from our house. After years of commuting by train to New York, he finally gets to sleep a little later in the mornings. And he finally gets to come home while there's light in the sky, a sight so incongruous half our neighbors lined up in front of our house just to see it, turning Mark's first few homecomings into impromptu cocktail parties.

I tiptoe downstairs to feed Jake, pour my coffee, and grab a bag of carrots for Eli. My lesson won't start for three hours, but I need to allow travel time and time for Eli to eat and digest his breakfast before I groom him and tack him up and put him to work.

Yeah, right. Who am I kidding? I just can't wait to ride him again.

Driving to Pegasus in the inky darkness, I marvel at the elusive X-factor that makes all the difference between a good ride and a bad one. Like other notoriously inconsistent sports—the game of golf comes to mind here—it's hard to believe that the same person who on some days can do nothing right, on others can do nothing wrong.

When everything works, I feel like there's nothing I can't sit to; as if I'm superglued to Eli's back. The reins feel like mere wisps of yarn, and I barely need to use my hands at all. I can let go and we still retain our connection. All I need is my seat and my legs.

I've tried visualization, physical and mental exercise, videos and more to hold on to the feeling of "feel." Nothing works; my good days are still few and far between, and I have no inkling of when a hot streak might end. At the same time, I know that the *occasional* good day is the first step on the long and winding road to consistency.

It's almost 6:30 when I pull into the parking lot, eager to see my beautiful horse. I make my way down the aisle by the early morning light that's just beginning to stream in through the skylights.

I don't want to turn on the overhead lights and rouse the others, since I'm only going to be feeding mine. I scoop Eli's morning grain into a bucket in the feed room and head for his stall. My eyes have adjusted to the dim light by now; I can just make out his silhouette.

It looks wrong.

I slide open his door for a better look, and as I do, I can see that he's balanced on the tripod of his front legs and his nose; his muzzle is half-buried in his shavings. His hind end appears to be jammed up against the back wall. As he lifts his head and tries to come toward me, he lurches forward, sways, and crashes into the side wall.

I'm already running down the aisle toward Mike's trailer behind the barn, Eli's grain flying out of the bucket that's still in my hand. I drop it and pound on the door with both fists. "*Mike,* wake up! Please come quick! There's something terribly wrong with my horse! Hurry!"

I hear muffled voices and realize he isn't alone, but I'm light years beyond caring, too frightened and alarmed by what I've just seen. "Yeah, okay," he calls. "I'll be there in a minute."

I run back to Eli, who has once again assumed his three-point stance, his unstable back end swaying. I tell him help is on the way, not to worry, just try to relax, though I'm sure my demeanor is anything but reassuring.

It takes Mike forever—three or four minutes at least—to make his way down the aisle to Eli's stall. I have the door open and I'm crouched in the shavings on the floor. "He looks like he's had a stroke," I say, choking back tears.

Mike watches Eli for a minute without saying a word. Then: "Let's check his vitals," he says. We take his temperature, check his pulse, count his breaths, listen for gut sounds, press on his gums to test capillary refill time, and pinch the skin on his neck to check for dehydration. The fact that everything's normal makes me feel no less frantic.

"He doesn't seem to be in any distress," Mike says.

"Then what *is* this? Have you ever seen it before? I rode him *yesterday.* He was *fine.*"

"You know what? I'll bet it's EPM. How much you want to bet?" Mike reaches in the back pocket of his jeans for his cell phone. "Let's wake someone up and find out."

While he summons the vet, I go outside and call Mark, who hears the fear in my voice and immediately offers to come up and wait with me. Much as I love him for it, I ask him to go home at noon and let Jake out instead, since I'll undoubtedly be here for a while. I promise to call back with an update as soon as I know anything at all.

Mike stays with us for the better part of the long and excruciating morning as we wait for the group practice down the road to send help. I'm hoping for a horse ambulance and a grizzled team of senior surgeons and been-there-done-that neurologists. Instead, they send me a weanling: Doogie Howser, DVM. As he comes sauntering down the aisle eating a bagel, flanked by an entourage like some baby rock star, all I want is for it to be yesterday.

He wipes his hand on his jeans and sticks it out for me to shake, introducing himself as Dr. Bob Neff. That done, Mike and I get down to business answering his questions. "Let's pull him out and do a neurological," says Dr. Neff to one of his backup singers, who clips a lead rope to Eli's halter. With another vet tech holding his tail to help steady him, they lead my sick, stumbling horse out of his stall and onto the aisle where, if such a thing is possible, he looks even worse.

"Okay, scratch that. Let's put him back in." Dr. Neff proceeds to hook Eli up to a giant IV bag filled with pyrimethamine-sulfonamide and dimethyl sulfoxide, an analgesic and anti-inflammatory, and a carrying agent for other drugs as well. A commercial solvent with a fifty-year history as a pharmaceutical agent, DMSO is commonly found in horse barns, where it's valued for its ability to penetrate skin without damaging it, making it a highly effective drug delivery system. It's also a smelly one, immediately announcing its presence with a strong garlic odor.

As the medicine goes to work, drip by drip, Dr. Neff tells me more about the mysterious illness suspected of attacking my horse and robbing him of his coordination overnight. Equine protozoal myeloencephalitis—EPM as it is commonly known—is a disease of the central nervous system caused by one of two single-celled parasites spread via the feces of infected possums, contaminating hay, grass, or grain.

Ingested by horses, the parasites multiply in the intestinal tract and are transmitted via the blood to the cells of the central nervous system, where they multiply and spread, killing the host cells as they exit, a process that can take anywhere from two weeks to two years.

Acute clinical signs like Eli's that appear overnight are among the hallmarks of EPM, though the disease can mimic a number of other neurological illnesses, making it difficult to diagnose.

Although many horses get exposed to the parasite, the vast majority manage to fight it off without ever showing any signs of disease. In the United States, less than one-half of 1 percent—fourteen new cases per 10,000 horses—are diagnosed annually, a highly exclusive club that I have no desire for Eli to join.

Stress caused by illness, exercise, or travel, to name but a few potential triggers, can suddenly bring on severe symptoms in horses that have been carrying the organism for months. Thinking back on our recent lessons and wondering if they're to blame, I'm feeling more than a little sick myself.

I take a molded plastic chair from the office and place it just inside Eli's stall, close enough so that I can reach over and touch him but not so close as to crowd him. There I sit for the rest of the day, watching the IV bag empty, drip by drip, into his neck.

Miracle of miracles: by evening he looks almost normal. I can only conclude that the medicines must be working, reducing the inflammation in his spine. Still, I'm afraid to go home. What if he worsens during the night? What if he panics? What if he falls? What if he goes down and can't get back up?

What if he dies?

What if he dies?

I feel the weight of something crushing my chest, something leaden that's making it hard for me to breathe; something frightening yet somehow familiar. Like a game-show contestant, I struggle to name the source before the buzzer sounds and I run out of time. *No, wait! I KNOW this one!*

Loss. The same feeling that lingered for weeks in the aftermath of each miscarriage, when my brain couldn't stop obliterating the people I love, tearing them out of the picture the minute they were out of my sight. Mark, driving off for an outing with Jake. My sister, taking the kids to the beach. I'd envision them gone for good, panic, and think: *That's how fragile life is.*

I had to be ready. I had to rehearse. Better that than be caught by surprise.

And that was the problem: I hadn't prepared. I forgot to rehearse losing my horse. I'd taken for granted that he'd be here for me, mitigating my childlessness and equalizing my grief; leading me out of my dark, quiet house and into the bright light of day.

* ⋆ *

ONE OF THE BENEFITS of having spent twenty-two years as an AP reporter is that I have absolutely no qualms about tracking down the world's leading experts on a given subject and getting them on the phone. I look up the numbers for some of the top veterinary schools in America and start working my way down the list.

At the Maxwell H. Gluck Equine Research Center at the University of Kentucky in Lexington, the epicenter of the Thoroughbred universe, I find a sympathetic researcher who listens without interruption as I lay out the facts of Eli's case.

As sick as he seemed that first morning, I learn that he could have been sicker still. Some EPM horses have difficulty swallowing. Some suffer seizures. Some collapse. The muscles of the eyes, face, and front limbs can become paralyzed. Horses can lose sensation in their bodies or necks. Severe signs of EPM include blindness, one-sided muscle atrophy, depression, and an inability to stand. I feel like crying just listening to the list of symptoms.

The researcher then tells me something invaluable: The state-of-the-art treatment for EPM in America, pyrimethamine-sulfonamide, an anti-malarial, does not, in fact, kill the parasite that causes the disease. What it *may* do is relieve the symptoms temporarily and depress the organism's viability, enabling the horse's immune system to control the infection during the treatment period. But once it's over, the symptoms can return.

"Isn't there anything that's more effective?" I ask. The lengthy pause on the other end gives me hope.

"There *is* an experimental treatment. It's a chicken-feed additive that's believed to kill the parasite. But it's not available in this country, at least not yet."

"What's it called? And where do I get it?" In my mind, I'm already throwing clothes in a suitcase, preparing to go wherever this stuff can be found.

"Bayer Laboratories in Canada."

"Great! I have relatives up there. Can they pick it up and send it to me?" I'm having a little trouble picturing my cousins, Neil and Doris, knocking on the door of Bayer Laboratories and requesting a jug of their finest chicken-feed additive to go. Maybe not.

Silence. Then: "You didn't hear this from me," says the researcher, "but for compassionate reasons, your vet can petition the FDA [Food and Drug Administration] for permission to bring it into the country to treat your horse's EPM."

"How do we do that? Can you walk me through it?"

By the time we hang up, I have all the information my vet needs to draw up the petition. Before the FDA can act on it, I'm required to sign a statement promising I will not eat my horse.

Because Eli's already several days into the conventional treatment, we have to wait till he's completed it before starting him on the experimental one.

By virtue of the fact that he lives at the barn, Mike takes on the unenviable chore of giving my horse his nightly dose of meds. After the first couple of times, Eli turns his back and tries to hide from his medicine in the far corner of his stall. But once he realizes that resistance is futile, Mike reports, Eli ultimately takes it like a man. I'm grateful that it's Mike and not me performing this particular wrestling match, given the impossible geometry of the length of my arms versus the length of Eli's neck.

Following doctor's orders, I won't be able to ride until after we're done with both treatments. Even though, for the most part, Eli looks and acts fine, he may very well get worse before he gets better, since a worsening of clinical signs can occur two weeks into treatment when the horse begins to shed the killed organism. Even if that doesn't happen, the less stress he experiences, the better. Rather than take any chances, the two of us spend quality time.

Although I miss riding, I can't say that I miss the tension and negativity that goes hand in hand with my training with Karen.

I decide to use this downtime to work on myself. I read a library's worth of books about dressage training and sports psychology. I watch others' lessons and try to learn along with them. I have a number of soul-baring conversations with Karen, who cheerfully refuses to entertain the idea that her bullying style could be in any way a contributing factor in my inability to relax on my horse.

"And so what if it is?" she says. "This is how I teach."

In other words, take it or leave it.

At the moment, I'm happy to leave it. There's an added fringe benefit to just hanging out with my horse, a kind of peace that I feel when I'm with him, asking nothing except his company in return.

After our morning walk, we hang out in the indoor, which is large enough to accommodate both riders and spectators. Eli takes to parking his head on top of mine; I'm the perfect height to serve as his chin rest. Every now and then, he nods off. I can tell by his deep, rhythmic breathing and the rapidly growing weight of his head. I rouse him gently when it gets to be too much.

By the time he's completed both courses of meds, I feel more in tune with him than ever. What began with a terrifying loss of control of his hind limbs ends two months later with a spinal tap, an invasive and expensive procedure that's almost as frightening as the disease that it tests for. With Eli heavily tranquilized but still standing, young Dr. Neff will insert an eight-inch-long needle into his spinal column and withdraw cerebral spinal fluid to check for antibodies.

There are obvious drawbacks to the spinal tap. For one thing, it can be difficult to get a clean sample of spinal fluid, and even a minute amount of blood will contaminate it, resulting in a false positive. And because the test is done with the horse awake and standing, however doped up he may be, there's always a chance that the animal will startle and jump as the needle goes in, endangering not only himself but the person holding the other end.

As I lead Eli down the aisle to the far end of the barn where his lower back will be sterilized and shaved and the procedure performed, Dr. Neff, the genius to whom I owe my horse's life, makes an unusual request: Could I please go away and not watch?

"Seriously?"

Peering down at me from the enormous box on which he is standing in order to be higher than Eli's spinal cord, he suddenly seems alarmingly vulnerable and defenseless. "So far, I've done ten of these, and all ten have gone well. It's not that I'm superstitious or anything, but this is nerve-wracking enough without having the owner looking on."

So I tell him I understand, and I give Eli a pat on the neck and tell him to be a good boy. I then wish both of them luck and disappear around the corner, out of sight but still within shouting distance just in case, God forbid, something goes wrong.

Nothing does. Within minutes, our intrepid vet is eleven for eleven. And after months of inactivity and terrible-tasting medicines, Eli is given a clean bill of health. His cerebral spinal fluid comes back without any sign of the parasite that nearly killed him.

Whereas he fully recovers, a part of me never quite does. I will never again take his health for granted, regardless of how robust he may seem. And I will never again say good-bye and drive off without turning back for one last loving look.

ten

JUNE 1999

$\mathcal{L}$ITTLE BY LITTLE THE WARM WEATHER RETURNS, and with it, my convalescing horse's strength. I switch from my winter "office" at the all-night diner off the highway to my summer quarters, a picnic table behind the barn, where I begin work on a book of essays about married life.

Looking on from his paddock as I write, Eli works his way through flake after flake of hay as I turn out page after page. Having him near me while I work is the next best thing to having him in my own backyard. It's a nice fantasy, one that I've had since I bought him. I can't see it happening, though. The zoning board would object, as would Jake, not to mention my neighbors (the grownups, at least).

Although Pegasus is situated just off a busy road minutes away from Starbucks and The Gap, I find it easy to forget the shopping centers and condo complexes the minute

I turn off and head down the dirt road. With its neatly fenced paddocks and horse-dotted pastures, Pegasus looks and feels like the country, the genuine article as opposed to the "exurbs" that pass for the country in more and more places these days.

The thriving farm stand across the road from the barn adds to the bucolic flavor, selling vegetables from a garden that looks like a commercial for Miracle-Gro. As a special treat, I sometimes wander over to buy Eli bunches of carrots with the dirt they grew in still clinging to them.

Among Pegasus's best features is its expansive front lawn, where Eli and I like to hang out on nice days. Although some of my fellow horsewomen equate grazing a horse to watching grass grow, I must respectfully disagree. Like watching him run, watching Eli eat grass puts me squarely in *his* world for a change, as opposed to me dragging him into mine.

Paradise to a horse is a lush pasture of timothy, the gold standard when it comes to grass hays, but almost any grass that's young, green, and fragrant will do in a pinch.

From watching Eli, I've discovered how inherently complex the seemingly simple activity of grass eating truly is. I see his prehensile upper lip sorting swiftly through the debris, pushing aside dirt, grit, twigs, and stems in favor of the short young grasses. I then watch it gather the blades in a neat little bundle for his upper and lower incisors to shear off.

Given the right vantage point, I catch the occasional glimpse of his tongue as it moves the neatly mowed grass to the cheek teeth on one side of his mouth. Like a Cuisinart, his teeth grind and chop it all into a big, grassy, slobbery cigar that he swallows even as he takes his next bite, once again sorting through the debris and moving the fresh blades to the *opposite* side of his mouth, alternating with every bite.

And so it goes, his steady rhythm interrupted only by the occasional drama: the unfortunate bumblebee eaten along with the grass, or the odd bad-tasting mouthful, ejected swiftly and emphatically back onto the lawn, every blade of it. And though Eli enjoys the bitterness of the occasional dandelion, he *knows* not to eat the buttercups, which are poisonous. Every now and then, he likes to cleanse his palate with a bite or two of dirt.

I understand the allure of grass a lot better, having watched an expert grazer in action. Even I can see that some grasses taste better than others, that tender beats tough every time. And that the grass really *is* always greener on the other side of the fence. It actually looks that way now to me, too.

It's also longer, which is why horses behind fences are forever contorting themselves to try to get at that tall, narrow, maddening strip just out of reach under the fence.

If managed extremely well, a single horse can be kept on as little as an acre of grass, though you really have to know what you're doing. The average horse can chew his way through close to thirty acres a year, churning much of it into mud in the process.

Not only is mud bad for a horse's feet, both in terms of lost shoes and the abrasive particles that can break down the skin's protective barriers and allow bacteria to enter, it's also slippery. That makes it dangerous for horses that like to run, as virtually all horses do. Mud also breeds bacteria and flies, causes soil compaction, discourages grass growth, and attracts weeds. Fortunately, none of this applies to the big lawn at Pegasus because horses are never turned loose on it; that is, not on purpose.

Watching Eli mow the front lawn, I am so entertained that it often takes me a while to notice on those occasions when we're no longer alone.

If not Greta, Eli's loyal groupie, it's almost always some other little girl with similarly shining eyes and sparkly nail polish who has persuaded a parent or, more likely, a grandparent to walk across the road from the farm stand. The girl in question is usually struck dumb by her proximity to An Actual Horse, leaving it to her grandmother to ask if it would be all right for her to say hi.

"Of course," I reply. "Come right over here next to me. He can't see you if you stand in front of him because of the way his eyes are placed on either side of his head. Do you want to pat him? Yes? Here, pat his neck, like this."

"What's his name?" The faintest whisper.

"Eli."

"It's a beautiful horse," Grandma offers from a safe distance away.

"I'm getting my own horse," says the girl, "as soon as I grow up."

"Good for you. That's exactly what I did."

Grandma: "Okay, time to go now. Say thank you to the lady."

At the rate of three or four such encounters a month, I wonder how many kids can count Eli as the first horse they ever saw up close, the first horse they ever actually touched.

* * *

THE SAME INTELLECT AND INQUISITIVENESS that make Eli easy to train and a joy to be with also compel him to investigate every potential hazard he sees. From idle machinery to broken fence rails, Eli never met a dangerous object he didn't want to get to know on a more intimate basis. As a result, he's hardly ever without a scrape, a cut, or a bruise.

Sometimes klutziness rather than curiosity gets the better of him, as it apparently did the day he finally got his turn to go out in the big field, as opposed to his usual sand paddock. I wasn't there to see it, but he must have had quite a time, given the fact that he went out wearing four shoes and returned wearing two. I considered it a minor miracle that I was able to find both in grass that was up to my knees. Horseshoes are expensive and, therefore, worth hunting for. So are cell phones, like the one I lost in the field while searching for Eli's shoes.

One morning I arrive to find Eli's right eye swollen shut. Another, I find virtually every inch of him covered in hives so enormous, he looks as though he's wearing bubble wrap.

If only he could.

Unsightly as they are, the hives don't seem to bother Eli anywhere near as much as they bother me. I strip his stall and swap straw for his usual pine shavings; I wash all his clothes, towels, wraps, and pads in hypoallergenic detergent. I weed-whack his paddock. I move him to a different paddock. Nothing helps, short of a brief course of dexamethazone, a corticosteroid that works by reducing inflammation (good) and suppressing his immune system (bad).

No matter what I try, the hives return again and again, whenever he completes another short course of steroids.

I eventually run out of things I can change in his immediate environment. And so, in desperation, I finally hire a veterinary dermatologist who sticks Eli with sixty-odd needles in a neat grid formation on his neck, testing his sensitivity to everything from feeds to weeds.

She finds three major allergens: cats, bugs, and dandelions, all of them fixtures at every barn in North America, if not the world. But by injecting him with these allergens, beginning with weak concentrations and gradually working our way up, we're able to banish the bulk of the hives, turning a chronic nuisance into an occasional one.

Other frustrating ailments continue to dog us, however. Scratches, also known as Mud Fever, a type of dermatitis to which horses with white legs (and muddy paddocks) are especially prone, produces scabby cracks and painful sores on Eli's one white stocking. Thrush, a fungal infection, settles into the crack between the bulbs of his heel. Although far from unusual, especially during the spring, when heavy rains transform sand paddocks into seas of mud, these conditions are no less painful or persistent for their ubiquity.

Given his sensitivity to these and other relatively minor maladies, along with his proclivity for coming down with them, Eli develops a bit of a reputation as a "hard keeper," one that is not, alas, entirely undeserved. I feel a kinship with mothers of rowdy young boys for whom the emergency room becomes a second home.

At the same time, I know better by now than to summon the vet for every minor cut or scrape, every slight fever or transient lameness. Like most horse owners, I've learned to take care of the small stuff myself. I can hardly afford to do otherwise. As it is, I suspect our vet bills have already broken some sort of single-horse record. I fully expect to see Eli's name on a new wing at the horse hospital any day now.

En route to my barn, I pass the so-called easy keepers in their fields, happy, healthy horses with shaggy coats and a layer of fat despite minimal supervision, and wonder where I might find a protective bubble large enough to encase mine.

All of this gets put into perspective in a hurry the morning I arrive to find a cluster of people huddled around a horse a few stalls down from Eli's, a horse that's inexplicably lying down in his stall despite frantic efforts to get him back on his feet.

Horses are engineered to spend most of their time on their feet. They even have a locking mechanism in their legs that keeps them from falling over when they're asleep. Although they do lie down briefly to sleep deeply or bathe in the sun, they can't do so for long periods without cutting off blood flow to vital organs and interfering with their breathing and digestive systems. A horse lying down for an extended period, like the one in the stall down the aisle, constitutes a medical emergency.

Over the next hour or so, we take turns trying to pull, push, and coax the poor animal to his feet, but all we succeed in doing is exhausting him. Ultimately, his strength gives out and he gives up. By this time, the vet has arrived, but there is nothing for him to do but to put the poor horse out of his misery.

The young man whose horse this is, a first-time owner who only recently acquired the animal, spends the rest of the morning sitting in the stall sobbing, cradling his dead horse's head in his arms. It's one of the saddest days I've yet witnessed in the horse world—but it's about to turn markedly worse.

The underlying cause of the horse's demise turns out to be equine herpesvirus-1, a highly—some would say *ridiculously*—contagious virus spread by horse-to-horse contact, airborne droplets, or direct contact with pathogens carried on clothing, boots, or hands. There's no specific treatment for EHV-1, nor is there a vaccine to prevent it.

Many horses with EHV-1 develop only respiratory infections: fevers, runny noses, and lethargy. Others, for reasons no one has been able to explain, develop severe neurological symptoms after a mutated form of the virus enters the spinal fluid and damages blood vessels in the brain and spinal cord.

The first sign is a fever, which the dead horse had had, followed a few days later by neurological signs. An inability to stand is one of them, as is lack of coordination, hind-end weakness, and a nasal discharge. If caught early and treated aggressively, horses with EHV-1 can recover, but many die.

Those that remain standing have a far better chance than down horses. But even though horses that stay down for more than twenty-four hours have very low survival rates, a few have fully recovered after having been down for as long as three weeks.

Some horses with neurological EHV-1 show no signs of the disease at all, yet they go on to infect other horses. A horse can also harbor the virus, only to have it recur under stress, making outbreaks difficult to prevent. The virus can live on inanimate objects like feed buckets and saddles for several days. It can also be spread from barn to barn on boots and clothing.

Those of us who tried to help the infected horse stand have most likely already carried the virus back to our own horses.

All we can now do is wait.

Still, just to feel like I'm doing *something*, I scrub every inch of Eli's stall with bleach, and I pray as our barn is placed under quarantine: no horses in or out for thirty days, a seemingly endless month of worry, not only for me but for everyone whose horses breathe the same air.

Miraculously, we all come through it unscathed.

* ⋆ *

BACK IN THE ALTERNATE (NON-HORSEY) UNIVERSE, my family and friends must think me deranged when they ask how Eli is doing and I answer them honestly. It's not hard to imagine what must go through their minds as I drone my way through our litany of ailments, from parasites in the spinal cord to giant bubble-wrap hives; from crippling abscesses to deadly airborne viruses.

Sometimes I don't have to imagine, like the day I'm on the phone with my sister in Los Angeles describing Eli's latest episode of foot soreness and she responds by asking, "Is this typical of horses? Or do you think it's possible you just got a lemon?"

Even though I am well aware that Eli and I have had more than our share of bad luck, her questions get my hackles up. "I'm not saying I did 'get a lemon,' as you so sensitively put it, but so what if I did? It's not like I'm going to drive him back to the dealer and trade him in like some lousy used car."

"No, but maybe you could find someone to take him," she says.

And with that, she has crossed the line. I am officially hurt. "Your kids aren't perfect either," I reply in my snottiest tone. "Would you consider giving them away?"

On that note, I hang up without giving her a chance to enumerate all the reasons this is a bogus comparison.

So, okay, I'm still sensitive about the childlessness issue, still touchy about the role Eli plays in my life and the shape of the empty place he fills. I'm also obviously more than a little defensive about my ability to care for him. The jury's still out, after all, on what sort of mother I would have made, had I been given the chance to find out.

Not that I spend all my spare time ruminating about such things. Thanks largely to Eli, I've come a long way since the days when I used to clip stories from the New York tabloids about abused and neglected children as evidence that regardless of whoever—or whatever—was responsible for its design, the system for allocating babies is, to say the least, flawed.

I collected numbers, too, for a time: ratios of eggs laid (huge numbers) to eggs hatched (tiny numbers) in a host of other species. This was evidence of another kind, evidence that my inability to carry a fetus to term was not caused by some personal failing but rather by the laws of nature that govern us all.

Not that I ever believed this, not entirely, but I've come to recognize and appreciate it for what it was: a message of love and encouragement to the depressed, hopeless me from the stronger, healthier part of myself.

For years, I kept this stuff hidden away in the baby book my next-door neighbor had given me after I'd confided I was pregnant for the first time, before I knew better than to make such premature pronouncements.

The book, with "A Tale of Baby's Days" on the cover, also served as the repository for printouts of my first-trimester ultrasounds, which were mostly pictures of empty gestational sacs. There was one, though, with a perfect little bean floating inside, and the beating heart that I actually saw on the screen; the one healthy baby my doctor promised I'd have, until it went the way of its vanishing twin.

Although I experienced considerable anguish over my failure to reproduce, on another level, I wasn't all that surprised. It merely confirmed what I'd known all along: that there was something fundamentally wrong with me, that I was deeply and irreparably flawed. By the time I'd lost my final pregnancy—the twins—I could no longer see the point of continuing to try. It had been my third strike, after all.

For a time, though I ended my treatment, infertility continued to dominate my life, delineating my thoughts and determining my friendships. As long as I continued to think about the babies I could never have, and as long as I continued to talk about them with others who could not have them either, it wasn't over. No one could accuse me of having thrown in the towel, technically speaking at least.

In screening candidates for the infertility breakfast support group I put together, I was careful to choose only the longest of long shots, women whose chances of delivering healthy babies hovered between slim and none. With the help of my local branch of Resolve, the national infertility association, I managed to come up with a most unpromising lineup: Betsy, who had yet to conceive after fourteen years and five in vitro fertilization cycles; Roberta, who'd miscarried her one and only pregnancy seventeen years before; and Sandy, whose endometriosis, along with her husband's low sperm count, made parenthood a pipe dream at best. Cindy, the fourth member, was pushing forty-five and had only one ovary. At long last, I had found the other members of my tribe.

Roberta was the first to get pregnant, closely followed by Betsy. Sandy was next. By the time we'd had our sixth monthly breakfast, my support system was down to two members, and I'd garnered a reputation as the woman whose hand infertile women most wanted to touch in order to finally conceive.

After a grim little breakfast with just the two of us, Cindy and I agreed to disband. For the sake of my karma, I managed one visit each with the three charter members after they'd all given birth. I also continued to attend every baby shower to which I was invited. If there was one thing I knew how to do by this time, it was how to buy fabulous gifts.

When my sister-in-law was about to deliver her second child, following a series of miscarriages that had run concurrently with mine, I even hosted her baby shower, decorating my living room with the same spray roses and colorful wooden blocks I'd once fantasized about having at mine.

Although I'd had no problem maintaining my composure as the hostess, unexpected baby sightings continued to throw me for a loop. Years after I'd disbanded my support group, I spotted Sandy in the checkout line at the Blockbuster video store, hugely pregnant and holding a toddler by the hand. I hid in Horror until they were gone.

And that was pretty much that, except for one little ritual I indulged in for more years than I'd care to admit. Each Mother's Day, I'd retrieve the baby book from its hiding place and revisit the scant remnants of my broken dreams: a half-dozen sympathy cards, a handful of dried flower petals, and a reminder for an ob-gyn appointment that never took place. I finally put an end to the whole macabre business, because life goes on and because ultra-sound images eventually fade. The last time I looked, I could no longer see the little bean.

The scars, though, are another matter. Faded now, they're by no means gone. Defects don't just go away. Mine have given me something to prove, and Eli remains my last, best chance to prove it. I could no more give him away than I could hand over my own beating heart.

Karen, though, has recently done just that: given her Thoroughbred away. She did it because he was getting on in years and was no longer physically able to give her every-thing she wanted from him. It's not for me to say whether she did the right thing, though I find myself struggling with the choice that she made. I keep envisioning a tribal elder drifting away on an ice floe. It's not the same thing, I realize. But still.

I'm aware that I lack a certain perspective, the one that comes of having owned more than one horse.

Reliable statistics on unwanted horses do not exist, but the US Department of Agriculture puts the number of horses sent to slaughter in Mexico and Canada each year at somewhere between 90,000 and 100,000. Clearly, the total number of unwanted horses is considerably bigger than this. *Horse Journal* estimates that 170,000 horses become un-wanted every year.

Even horses that *are* loved and wanted change hands. Children outgrow their ponies. Professionals train "green-ies" and resell them at a profit. Recreational riders retire aging mounts in order to afford younger ones. There are a number of retirement homes for these old pensioners, farms where they can spend whatever time they have left running with a herd and living as nature intends.

Others aren't as lucky, as their physical and behavioral baggage attests. Many horses are starved or beaten, or both, left in stalls without food or clean water, or made to stand in their own manure for weeks, their untrimmed hooves curling up at the toe like elf slippers. Even well-intentioned enthusiasts can and do make poor choices, and end up with horses they're ill-equipped to handle. The bottom line is that horses make very poor impulse purchases, and as such, they are particularly vulnerable to abuse and neglect.

A bad economy is also hard on horses. First-time owners who don't know what they're getting themselves into can quickly become disenchanted with the high cost, hard work, and long hours associated with horse ownership. Because horses are such expensive mistakes, they often end up abandoned in someone else's pasture. Others end their lives at slaughterhouses, having been sold by the pound.

For these and other reasons, many horses don't get to live out their lives with their original owners. Many don't get to live out their lives at all.

A small minority in America still work for a living, patrolling neighborhoods, pulling carriages in cities, or rounding up cattle in the West. But for the most part, horses are high-ticket luxuries, among the first to go in hard times and the last to return in better ones, women being the primary spenders on horse-related goods and the least likely to put their own (horse-related) needs ahead of their families'. This is bad news for the nearly 5 million Americans involved in the horse industry.

Even in prosperous times, for all but the wealthiest, horse ownership can be a real stretch. I've already cobbled together a list of the worldly possessions I'd sell before parting with Eli, right up to and including my house. In all fairness, though, it wouldn't just be my decision. There's also my spouse, whose income and generosity are in large part how I've been able to afford Eli in the first place.

And though I went into this with a certain feeling of entitlement—my strongly held belief that I deserved to have something, some*one* to nurture—I have to concede that my husband, Eli's primary benefactor, gets little or nothing in return for his largesse, aside from a happier wife.

Some days—especially lately—he doesn't even get that.

eleven

AUGUST 1999

PEGASUS IS A BUSY PLACE IN THE SUMMER, with day camp during the week and gymkhanas on weekends, when the parking lot becomes clogged with horse trailers. The outdoor riding ring has a judges' reviewing stand on one of the long sides that gets plenty of use. (No matter how many times we uneventfully pass it, Eli continues to eye it warily, convinced that it houses a monster.)

I find myself getting up earlier than ever to squeeze in a lesson or a ride ahead of the crush. Then Eli and I are free to hang out on the front lawn, where Eli grazes and I people-watch.

My favorites are the middle-aged men who pull up in their minivans, don their chaps, and saddle their Quarter Horses to become instant suburban cowboys, the walk, the mannerisms, and the lexicon all there.

All hat, no cattle? If only that were the case. The baby steers that Mike acquires for roping practice are housed in the round pen behind the barn, keening in muddy misery and striking terror in the hearts of the horses, mine included. Simply leading Eli past them becomes a daily adventure. I'm not sure which one of the cowboys had the bright idea to buy a tool and castrate the steers himself. I just thank God I wasn't there to see or hear it.

In addition to a boarding barn, Pegasus is also a dumping ground for unwanted animals of all kinds, some of which vanish as abruptly as they appeared. Clarence, the guinea fowl that dive-bombed me daily during the summer I spent at the picnic table writing my book, disappears one day without a trace. Come to think of it, though, his disappearance may have been less of a mystery than most, since he'd developed the unfortunate habit of pecking at the backs of the horses' legs while they were being ridden.

Goats, cats, and rabbits also find their way to Pegasus, along with an orphaned spotted fawn. There's no such thing as an unwanted animal to Mike, who loves and embraces them all. Not surprisingly, word gets around.

Although nobody's pet, Pegasus's unofficial mascot this summer is a very large, very smart toad that spends evenings in front of the soda machine, gorging on insects attracted to the light.

Like Eli, I, too, am allergic to felines, which is why I do my best to ignore the cats at the barn. I succeed with all but one, the gray-and-white male we call Max, the Cat That Will Not Be Ignored. Max thinks nothing of launching himself into my arms or climbing my leg as if it were a tree. Because he demands love and refuses to take no for an answer, I love him in spite of myself.

Max's specialty is stowing away in people's cars, and he happens to be very good at it. Many times I'd be doing seventy on the interstate, well on my way home, when he'd suddenly surface and scare the crap out of me.

It's a sad day at Pegasus when Max finally disappears for good, though I'd like to believe he finally found his ride home. When I think of him now, I picture him spending the rest of his days on a sofa next to a fireplace as opposed to a drafty barn, living on proper cat food instead of dead mice.

Of course, there are plenty of other, nondomesticated animals around: A family of foxes, deer by the dozens, the occasional snake, and the usual complement of barn rats, barn swallows, and chipmunks. One day, we discover a nest of baby mice in the far corner of a stall, carefully watched over by a draft horse weighing in at over a ton.

We also have raccoons, those little masked bandits of the night, some of them apparently not so little. More than once I arrive to find the contents of my brush box strewn across the barn floor with a formerly full bag of Eli's molasses cookies chewed through, cookies gone; a hole in his bag of carrots, teeth marks in some, others rejected; the trash can on its side, food wrappers flung about, contents empty, and so on. All evidence points to something with hands.

Whatever it is, it's making Eli act squirrely. I find him huddled in the back of his stall, refusing to budge and showing the whites of his eyes, as horses do when they're nervous or spooked. Even carrots won't dislodge him.

I put on his halter, attach a lead rope and give it an I-mean-business tug. Nothing. It's like putting a leash on a bronze statue and expecting it to walk. I tack him up in his stall, sighing with impatience. With a bit in his mouth, he finally lets me lead him out.

After our ride, though, he still can't relax. He tries to back up on the cross ties, turning his head as if to look for something behind him. Although I assure him there's nothing there, and even go so far as to walk him around the barn to show him, he remains twitchy.

This same frustrating routine goes on for several days, long after I stop leaving food in the barn, right up until the day Eli spontaneously returns to normal. Whatever it is that's been upsetting him, it's apparently no longer an issue.

At times like these, I wish the barn were equipped with a surveillance camera. I would love to know exactly what had gone bump in the night.

* * *

BEING THE FIRST TO ARRIVE at a barn bestows upon the early bird horse-lover blessings too numerous to count, from the guttural greetings of the newly awakened to the harmonic chewing of the recently fed.

More important, though, it also means being the first to respond to equine emergencies large and small, from torn, tangled blankets to full-blown colic.

On one chilly morning at Pegasus, I walk in to the unmistakable sound of running water and follow my ears to a stall on the opposite side from Eli's, where I find a terrified, shivering mare up to her arthritic knees in her rapidly flooding stall. It doesn't take a detective to solve the mystery of what has occurred: she'd somehow managed to turn on the tap just outside her door that is used to fill her water buckets. She's only too happy to let me slip on a halter and lead her out of her lake and into a dry stall.

Eli maintains his habit of sounding the loose-horse alarm in barn after barn, pacing agitatedly back and forth in front of his various windows, refusing carrots and grain until I get the message and round up the escapee.

Sometimes I need only follow the trail of destruction to locate the responsible party, as when a loose horse has been wandering the barn, trampling blankets, toppling bales of hay, and leaving piles of manure in his wake.

I'm not the only one around, thank God, the morning a geriatric horse being led to a paddock slips and falls on his side on the ice. A half dozen of us push and pull to no avail; without traction, he keeps sliding back down. We try shoveling wood shavings onto the ice, but of course, they keep sliding away. I finally go into the barn and find a turnout rug that we slip underneath the old-timer's legs. With the rug in place, he's able to get back on his feet.

Another morning at another barn, I arrive at dawn to find an enormous tarp in the middle of the outdoor ring. My first reaction is mild annoyance. How am I going to ride my horse out there with whatever the hell that is in the way?

What *is* that? From the size of the tarp, I assume it's covering a piece of equipment, a tractor or maybe the rake used to even out the footing in the riding rings. As I walk over to get a better look, a breeze lifts a corner of the tarp and I see a hoof. My heart pounds.

I run back into the barn, checking stalls as I go. The empty one had been occupied by a new horse brought in on trial a couple of weeks before, a mare that had had issues with being cross tied on the aisle, requiring her to be groomed and tacked up while attached to a lead rope. As I find out later that morning, the horse had reared while being worked on the lunge line and had fallen over backward, dead the minute she hit the ground.

Because she was insured, an autopsy must be done. The vet comes out and performs it right where the poor horse is lying. After he's finished and the remains are taken away, no one has an easy time of it in the ring. Even after several of the boarders load bloody dirt into wheelbarrows and haul it away, the horses are freaked out for days, until a heavy rain finally washes the remnants away. The smell of blood is a perilous omen for horses, as well as a potentially life-saving one that triggers the fight-or-flight response. It's a wonder they didn't all head for the hills in the time it took for the odor to dissipate.

Although it was a grisly find, I am consoled knowing that at least the mare had been beyond suffering. That wasn't the case some years later when I arrived at yet another barn to find a young horse named Smarty in the throes of an acute colic attack.

Smarty was a relative newcomer, having been with us just under six months. An unusual-looking horse and a striking one, he stood out amid the chestnuts, bays, and grays, a Red Roan Overo Paint in a sea of Thoroughbreds, Quarter Horses, and warmbloods. Paint horses are so named because they resemble white horses that have been splattered with paint. Each one is different, each a unique work of art.

Smarty's splatters were deep reddish brown, flecked with white in irregular patches along his back, chest, the sides of his neck, and his right front leg. He had a white face, black-rimmed brown eyes, and the dark ears and poll celebrated in Native American culture as a legendary source of supernatural protection. Among some of the Plains tribes, horses with these so-called Medicine Hat markings were to be ridden only by tribal chiefs, medicine men, and great warriors.

What little I knew about Smarty I'd gleaned from having served him his breakfast four mornings a week: that he was feisty at mealtime and that he didn't much like being confined in a stall. That was hardly enough to prepare me for what I found when I arrived at the barn in the early morning hours two days before Christmas.

Smarty's stall had been trashed beyond anything I'd ever seen, an indication of his suffering as he'd thrashed and kicked his way through the night. It's hard to describe just how terrible a colicky horse can look, locked away in a prison of pain with no awareness of anything else. I took one look and ran back to my car for my cell phone to wake up the barn owner, a woman named Beth.

As I waited with Smarty for her to arrive, I lost count of the number of times he threw himself down and got up again, rolling and pawing and kicking at his abdomen. I talked to him as calmly as I could, telling him help was coming and to hang on, but my words were more for my sake than his. He was beyond hearing.

Led outside, he immediately collapsed in the nearest snowbank. We let him lie there in the hopes that the snow would help numb the pain, as we waited for Shelly, his owner, and her vet.

Watching Smarty, I remembered my friend Susan's words on the night that was to be Frank's last: "The first horse you see put down shouldn't be a horse that you love." I began to shiver, and not only because I was up to my knees in a snowbank. "Maybe we should cover him with one of his blankets," I said to Beth, who went to fetch it. We were draping it over him when Shelly pulled up.

I knew her only slightly, having been at the barn on Smarty's first day as a boarder, a bright summer morning. Shelly and I had spent an hour or so chatting. She told me she'd bought Smarty as a four-year-old and that he'd caught her eye not only because of his flashy coat but because his natural markings included a thirty-two on his right hip and a heart on his right shoulder. "I was thirty-two when I first saw him, and our relationship was truly a heart-to-heart connection," Shelly said.

She was friendly and thoughtful, knowledgeable about horses and people, and I'd often wished our schedules were more compatible. As it was, I'd run into her only once or twice since.

As tactfully as possible, I described how I'd found Smarty that morning. There was no need for excruciating detail; his condition was plain to see. Shelly knelt in the snow alongside his head and stroked him gently, something he would never have held still for under normal circumstances. "He showed his affection in 'his' way," Shelly said later. "Traditional displays were few and far between."

This time, though, he didn't object. "I knew at that moment he was in big trouble and something was seriously wrong," she said.

The sick horse that lay in the snow bore little resemblance to the happy, contented one Shelly had said good night to just hours before. "He had an angelic look about him. I even saw a shiny dime on the cement floor on my way to the tack room, and I said, 'Smarty, our angels are here.' And they were."

He was already dying by the time the vet arrived. A portion of his intestines had ruptured, releasing toxins into his body; his grayish-blue gums telegraphed his decreased oxygen supply. Not even surgery could save him.

With the pain medicine the vet administered, Smarty managed to stand. Slowly and carefully, Shelly and her vet walked him to a flat area behind the barn for the other injection, the one that made him wobble and go down for the last time. He was ten, like the dime Shelly had found on the floor.

In their six years together, "Smarty taught me more than I'd learned in the previous twenty," she said. "He was very complex and a challenge, but I wish I'd had twenty more years with him."

Her horse, having died much too young, is buried in the gelding paddock beneath the turf he once grazed along with a half dozen others, all of them loved, all of them missed.

Each a unique work of art.

twelve

DECEMBER 1999

ℬAD WEATHER HAS KEPT ME AWAY from Pegasus for a week when I finally make the trip, accompanied by five pounds of carrots and immeasurable guilt. Not that there was anything I could've done to get there sooner. I can't control the weather, after all.

But even before I open the door to a chorus from the hungry horses inside, I know I have some explaining to do. Eli gives me the once-over before accepting a conciliatory carrot. He withholds his usual welcoming nicker, not that he needs to say a word. A horse's eyes are the largest of any land animal. His say it all: *Where the hell have you been?*

Sitting at home in front of my laptop checking the weather incessantly, that's where. It doesn't happen often, but every now and then over the course of a Connecticut winter comes a spate of days not fit for man or beast, woman or Volvo. We've just had one such stretch: ice and snow, rain and sleet, followed by more ice and more snow.

As is invariably the case when I'm away from him for more than a couple of days at a time, I'm struck by how quickly my horse starts to act like a *horse.*

A horse is a horse (of course, of course), and as such, mine will forever revert to type when provoked, flattening his ears, baring his teeth, and lifting a hind leg in warning. Similarly, when frightened, he will always and forever run first and ask questions later. But for the most part, the more time I spend with him, the more docile he seems to become. On occasion, I even catch myself thinking of him as a very large, very strong dog, a misguided notion to be sure.

When I'm not there, however, the bulk of his interactions are with members of his own species. Although horses do share a language ranging from blowing to sighing and from whinnying to nickering—punctuated by occasional squealing—they rely heavily on body language to communicate with others in the herd. Which is what I, myself, seem to be at the moment: Just another face in the crowd, though thankfully nowhere near as long as the rest.

FOR ANYONE IN THE SALT BELT who has unavoidable business outdoors, the first significant snowstorm of the year is always a game changer. No more spontaneous outings, no more clean getaways, no more firm plans without the caveat "weather permitting."

Tough as snow and ice can be, though, for my money, extreme cold is what separates the horse owner from the horse lover. Every January, there comes a night when I go to sleep in Connecticut and wake up in Siberia. Days with single-digit temperatures and below-zero wind chills are to horse owners as the sultriest summer days are to dog people: tens on the misery index.

Not so for horses. Having evolved in the northern regions of Europe and Asia, horses acclimate easily to the cold. Metabolic changes start to take place in late summer, when horses respond to the shortening daylight by growing a protective layer of fat and a denser hair coat, both of which trap body heat. Horses can maintain their normal body temperature, right around 100°F, in weather ranging from 15°F to 60°F without having to expend any additional energy.

Wind and wet weather are another story. Both can flatten the hair coat, eliminating its heat-trapping qualities, and though it takes a lot of rain or snow to soak a horse to the skin, once wet, a horse can lose body heat up to twenty times faster than a horse that's dry. Fortunately, both wind and wet can be overcome with a run-in shed, a three-sided structure that horses seeking shelter can enter and exit at will.

The frigid cold I'd been dreading since October—that numbing blast of Arctic air known to meteorologists as the Alberta Clipper—arrived overnight while I slept, accompanied by breathless weathermen and dead car batteries. The first thing I think of when I open my eyes is the thick film of ice that has undoubtedly formed on Eli's water bucket.

These brutally cold winter days tend to start far too early. My alarm goes off well before dawn to allow ample time for my Arctic chores: dressing in layers of thermals and fleece, scraping ice off my windshield and pre-heating my car for the hourlong drive north and east to Eli's barn.

The squeak of tires on snow keeps me company as I drive; the dark shadowy shapes of deer at the edge of the woods keep me alert. However tempted by the half dozen diners I pass, I make do with my thermos of coffee and drive on. Hungry horses are waiting.

The drive is beautiful this time of year, between the snow and the Christmas lights that are still burning. Ridgefield, the big town I drive through halfway there, is especially lovely, the downtown all dressed up in little white lights—the stores, the trees, the big old homes along the main street—giving it a magical air.

I know this drive—every bump, every crack, every bend—the way a bike-riding kid knows the sidewalks. I know precisely how long every traffic light stays yellow. I know every cop's hiding place. I can pinpoint the spots where the deer cross the road. Like Eli and me, they are creatures of habit. Not so the ducks or the geese, both of which occasionally stop traffic in more temperate weather as they lead their offspring from puddle to pond.

Horse farms still dot the main street in Eli's town, and there's one in particular that I always watch for: an old-fashioned red barn with a huge wreath of fresh greens illuminated by a spotlight, a perfect still life.

With the weather this cold, a spectacular sunrise is a given, and I feel lucky to get to see it so often. Hard as it was in the beginning to get up in the dark, Eli has transformed me into a morning person.

The horses in the windowed stalls keep a vigil for my Volvo, greeting me as I park my car and hurry through the dark toward their barn: My own horse's soft, friendly nicker—*Hey, over here!* The draft horse's giant hoof kicking his door—BAM! BAM! BAM! The anxious squeal of the

Paint, whose stall is around the back—*I'm out here! Don't forget about me!*

Their breakfasts are lined up and labeled in plastic pails set up the previous night. I stack them in order of who gets fed first and dump them into the appropriate feed buckets. Next, I toss a flake of hay into each stall and pause briefly to enjoy the music of contented chewing. After a quick pit stop, I hurry back to the car to warm up.

My hands ache with the cold just from coming in contact with the plastic pails; they feel worse before they feel better as I rub them vigorously in front of the heater. I glance at the paper but keep one eye on the barn.

Invariably, as I wait for my body to thaw, my thoughts drift back to the New Hampshire winters of my childhood, the ones that arrived in November and loitered into May, transforming the landscape into a blindingly white world where nothing, it seemed, could ever live again.

The severity and duration of those winters demanded that they be embraced. We faced them head-on with snowsuits, long underwear, and wool socks encased in plastic bags and fake fur-lined boots; with skates, skis, sleds, and flying saucers; with shovels, brooms, and huge bags of rock salt; with cocoa powder, canned soup, and grilled cheese.

I learned to approximate the temperature by the angle of rising chimney smoke, the squeak and crunch of the snow underfoot, and the formation and shape of the icicles that hung daggerlike from the roof line.

Today, with only my car heater and my coffee to warm me, I reluctantly turn off the engine and head back into the barn. Luckily, Eli is a pretty good heater, and by the time I'm through grooming him, I'll be able to peel off at least one layer. Warm as my body will be by the time I'm done riding, though, my feet will once again feel more like blocks of ice than like feet; my nose will run and my ears will be numb.

The rest of my family has long since escaped to the temperate climates of Southern California and South Florida. Not me. Cold as I am, I'm also oddly at home in this familiar, inhospitable setting, still facing winter head-on, still embracing its cruel, austere beauty.

* ⋆ *

IT'S HARD TO PINPOINT the precise moment an old wound finally heals, the first time you notice it's no longer hurting.

After the night Katie came to my house with strawberries, Champagne, and brie, I made a concerted effort to stop hiding inside. I started small: a friendly wave as I drove past the moms, or a quick chat when I walked Jake up the street.

Then I upped the ante a little at a time, reaching out with small gestures of friendship. When I heard that Amy was going stir-crazy recovering from surgery, I lent her some books and had her over for lunch. When Liz came home from the hospital, I made a welcome-home dinner for her and her visiting parents and delivered it to her door in the rain.

I got to know Nancy when she rescued a shelter dog and sought my advice about how best to train him; I made friends with Felicia, the mother of two rambunctious little boys, when she wandered, overwhelmed, down the street, seeking temporary refuge in my quiet, adult house.

That spring, just as the last of the snow finally melted, I heard a knock on the door and opened it to find Claire's son, Sam, and Nancy's son Colin out canvassing for cookies, a ritual they would repeat countless times over the years.

A week or two later, I happened to glance out the window just as Marcia's son, Matt, hit a bump and flew over the handlebars of his bike. I washed his scraped knees in my bathroom and felt downright heroic as I retrieved the SpongeBob SquarePants Band-Aids I'd been saving for just such an emergency.

Did my heartache end the Halloween I dressed the unceasingly tolerant Jake as a Dalmatian and brought him to the neighborhood party? Or was it the following one, when I stopped feeling the need to treat my dog like a child and was content to stay home and hand out the treats?

Either way, by the time Jake developed a full-blown thunderstorm phobia during the second half of his life, every one of my neighbors knew to check for my car in the driveway at first rumble and to come rescue Jake if I wasn't home.

And one summer night when we were out with Mark's parents watching the blue sky turn black, I called Claire in a panic and in lieu of hello she answered the phone with, "We've got him."

That may have been the pivotal moment—that, or the one shortly after, when I rushed into her living room to find Jake in a state of bliss, at the center of a ring of children all trying to hug him at once.

All I know for sure is that I woke up one day and the pain that had been so acute for so long wasn't there. Nor was my desire to move. I realized then that I'd been in the right place all along: home on Hickory Lane, where I belong.

* ⋆ *

I ARRIVE FOR MY EARLY MORNING LESSON with Karen feeling festive and optimistic. It's Christmas Eve—my favorite holiday just hours away—and I've brought Karen's present: a pair of silver earrings. I'd spent many hours shopping for them. I'm usually an excellent gift giver, but I've yet to buy Karen a present she likes. Everything I've ever given her she's handed back to me with the suggestion that I "try again," or words to that effect. Not this time. This time I'm confident I've finally gotten it right, and I can't wait to give them to her.

I pull Eli out of his stall, feed him his carrots, and groom him and put on his tack, keeping one eye on the clock. Like me, Karen tends to be punctual. With ten minutes to go, I bring Eli into the indoor, walk him around once and tighten his girth, then lead him to the mounting block.

I've just gotten on him when the front door opens and Karen slips inside. "Hey! Merry almost Christmas," I say, as we head toward her. She waves us off with a frown and says, "Keep him walking."

Damn, I think. *It's going to be one of* those *days.* They seemed to come with increasing regularity, though I never knew till the start of a lesson which kind of day it would be.

On a good day, she greets Eli and me warmly, and we chat a few minutes before we get down to work. Those few minutes, when all three of us are relaxed, tend to set the tone for the session to come, reducing the tension right from the start.

Unfortunately, the opposite is also true. I try again.

"I have your present," I say. "I think you're going to like this one."

"Huh," she says. "More weight right."

I try to shift my position, but I can already feel my defenses rushing to the fore, my muscles stiffening, my body awkwardly trying to compensate for my complete and utter lack of fluidity.

"Right shoulder back," she orders. "Today, not tomorrow."

I try to bring my right shoulder back, but it ain't happening.

"Uhhhh," she says, assuming an only slightly exaggerated version of my position: Igor, the hunchbacked laboratory assistant. "This is not putting your right shoulder back," she says.

I take a deep breath, let it out, and try to start over.

"Bigger walk."

I squeeze Eli's sides with my legs; he lengthens his stride, but not enough.

"Is your leg on him? Is it?"

I nod.

"Then kick the shit out of him!"

I give him a kick and he picks up a trot.

"Why is he trotting? I said walk!"

I close my fingers on the reins and he returns to a walk.

"Bigger walk!" Karen barks, right on cue.

So it goes for the better part of an hour.

Not surprisingly, she doesn't care for the earrings.

* * *

With New Year's Day fast approaching, I attempt to explain to Eli that we're about to enter a brand-new millennium, one that I sincerely hope will be injury and illness free. "Is that clear?" He bobs his head up and down, then wipes his mouth on my sweatshirt, leaving a trail of green slime. A warning sign? Perhaps.

Sure enough, Y2K brings a new problem: a severe yet migrating lameness with no apparent cause. After several inconclusive exams, the vet suggests I have a nuclear bone scan done on my horse. Mike offers to trailer us to the Hospital for Large Animals in North Grafton, Massachusetts, part of the Cummings School of Veterinary Medicine at Tufts University, home of the nearest bone scanner.

Although I'd prefer a non-hospital destination, as undoubtedly Eli would, too, I have to admit that traveling with my horse has a certain cachet. "Hey, guess what," I tell him. "You and I are taking a trip!" I pack for both of us, arranging to stay at a nearby hotel for the two nights that Eli will be in the hospital.

Mike's gooseneck six-horse trailer is a far cry from the modest two-horse one that brought us to Pegasus the previous winter. Comfortable, spacious, and new, the rig is the equine equivalent of a stretch limo. Smart horse that he is, Eli doesn't hesitate to follow Mike up the ramp to check out his posh new digs for the two-hour drive. I'm every bit as comfortable up front in Mike's truck, and the trip seems to take no time at all. Set off by white-fenced paddocks and surrounded by snow-covered hay- and cornfields, the veterinary complex looks to be in the middle of nowhere, and is. It occupies the grounds of a former state hospital farm colony listed on the National Register of Historic Places.

Human patients were grouped by behavior rather than diagnosis and housed accordingly; the "excited" were confined in brick buildings, the "peaceful," in unlocked cottages. Thelonious Monk was once held here for a week for observation before being discharged. "I can't be crazy," he famously said, "'cause they had me in one of those places and they let me go." No word on whether Monk was considered "peaceful" or "excited."

We follow the signs to the Large Animal Hospital, where Mike unloads Eli and leads him to a holding stall while I handle the paperwork. I do my best to hurry through it, since I can hear the shrill sound of my frantic horse whinnying for me from behind several sets of closed doors.

"Anything you need before I head back?"

I look up and see Mike with his keys in his hand. "I think we're all set. Thank you so much for bringing us. I'll call you as soon as I know when he's being discharged."

Watching him go, I now feel in charge of my horse in a way that I've never quite felt before. In the past, whenever I've summoned the vet for Eli, someone more senior has been there with me. With the notable exception of the heroic Dr. Neff, the vets we've dealt with have tended to address themselves to barn managers or trainers, as opposed to inexperienced owners who are merely there to write the checks.

Once, a few months after Zoe was born, my sister and I took her to a Christmas crafts show. With Debbie's blessing, I wore the Snugli with Zoe inside and accepted compliments as if she were mine. The charade fell apart the first time a woman asked me how much Zoe had weighed at birth. I looked to my sister, who answered without hesitation. Apparently no birth mother ever forgets the size of the baby she labored to push out. It was pretty clear who was the real mom and who was the impostor.

A similar feeling shadowed me throughout my first years with Eli, when others jumped in to respond to vets' questions while I struggled to formulate answers. Now, though I realize I still have a lot left to learn, it's kind of nice for a change not to have anyone question my authority with regard to my horse, or my ability to care for him.

It feels strange to be inside an actual building with Eli, "indoors," as opposed to a freezing, unheated barn. He won't need to wear his blanket or even a sheet while he's here. It's room temperature, a comfy 68°F.

Once I've moved Eli to his assigned stall on the medical ward, I pull out his curry comb, body brushes, and hoof pick and give him a thorough grooming, something that's normally difficult to do in the dead of winter. I like being able to scratch all his itchy spots, to feel his skin and look him over without some filthy blanket impeding my view. He looks pretty good—a little shaggy, of course, but that's to be expected. I can't wait to give him a nice, warm shower.

I meet the doctor and students assigned to our case and the vet tech whose job it is to jog Eli up and down the rubber-matted hallway while we watch him go, a scene vaguely reminiscent of my own near-naked run up and down the corridors of the Boston Children's Hospital three and a half decades ago.

Although it's a great luxury to have so many knowledgeable pairs of eyes trained on my horse, even I can see his stride is short on his right front leg, a chronic issue, as I explain to his team. Tomorrow he'll have the bone scan. I'm hoping it will give us some answers.

Back on the ward, I stay with Eli till he seems sleepy and reasonably relaxed. I hate to leave him, but he could probably do with some rest. He's had a big day and he'll have an even bigger one tomorrow. So I leave a five-pound bag of carrots outside his door, along with a note inviting anyone reading it to feed him. Then I tell him good night, reminding him I'll be back in the morning first thing, and head out to find my hotel twenty minutes away.

The next morning, I get up early and return to the hospital to the sight of Eli surrounded by students, all trying to coax him to eat his breakfast. Fortunately, the minute he sees me, he forgets all about his hunger strike and buries his face in his feed bucket.

I give him another good brushing and walk him up and down the rubber-matted hall, occasionally passing other women and horses doing the same thing. I can't imagine he got much sleep in this strange-smelling place filled with sick and injured horses and white-coated humans. Not that horses require much sleep: two or three hours will do, on average, over a twenty-four-hour period, most of it broken up into shorter naps.

I wonder what he'll make of the bone scan. I'd try to explain, but I barely understand it myself.

Too soon, someone comes to inject him with the radioactive dye that over the course of the next few hours will accumulate around any inflamed bones that could be contributing to his lameness. He'll then be scanned with a special camera that detects the signal from the isotope, producing an image that highlights any areas of inflammation.

I'm told I'll have to leave before Eli can be injected, so I rub his neck and tell him to be a good boy. Back at my hotel I'm too restless to pay attention to any of the books or magazines I've brought along. I'm talking to Mark on the phone when I happen to glance outside and see that it's snowing. The air is filled with small, relatively dry flakes—serious snow, as opposed to the big, wet postcard variety. I suddenly feel claustrophobia coming on, so I tell Mark I'll call him back a little later. I then pull on my boots and my coat and go outside.

There's nowhere to walk to—the hotel is right off the highway—so I circle the parking lot a few times and go back in. It's snowing like hell by this point, and I'm worried about road conditions. How am I going to get back to the hospital the next day if this keeps up? I can see the traffic on the highway and it looks like a formidable mess. Nothing appears to be moving.

When I call Tufts to check on Eli, I'm told the test went fine. Eli's back in his stall, but still too radioactive for me to visit. Also, the vet who's in charge of him is leaving tonight for a funeral in Pennsylvania and won't be back for a couple of days, so I might not get the results until he returns.

Either way, because of the radioactivity—which poses more of a health threat to me than to Eli, because he'll pee most of it out within twenty-four hours—we won't be able to leave until 5:00 PM the next day at the earliest, which means I probably won't get home until 10:00. In the meantime, Eli will need to pass a Geiger counter test before I can see him, which won't happen until midafternoon.

As long as he's already there, I'm also having the internist do a breathing test that will measure Eli's lung function and determine whether or not that's an issue. He suffered a minor bout of pneumonia before we moved to Pegasus, and he's been too easily winded ever since. It's a very sophisticated test that can only be done here, at Cornell, or at the University of Pennsylvania. It's not cheap, but then again, nothing is. At this point, I figure I might as well be hung for sheep as lamb. Prior to the bone scan, the technician had had to remove Eli's front shoes and my farrier is conveniently in Florida, so I have no idea when or how I'll get them back on. At the moment, though, that's fairly low on my list of worries.

I check the time and can't believe it's only 6:00 PM. It feels like midnight. I'd woken up obscenely early the previous day, afraid that I might oversleep, so naturally I barely slept at all. Mike had done the same thing. When I'd arrived at the barn at 5:30 yesterday morning, he had already hitched up the trailer and was ready to go.

Now that the trip's all but over and the necessary tests have been done, there's nothing left for me to do but to wait for the radioactive dye to dissipate so that Eli and I can go home. I finally chill out. I eat a burger and read, watch a movie and send a detailed e-mail to Eli's fans. By the time I wake up the next morning, the snow has stopped and the roads have been plowed. I have a leisurely breakfast, check out of my hotel, and drive back to Tufts to drop off the rental car, pay the four-figure hospital bill, and wait for Eli to stop glowing so that Mike can collect us.

First, though, I sit down with one of the doctors assigned to our case, who, after telling me what a nice horse I have, informs me that the bone scan is normal. Eli's case "is a real head-scratcher."

It's been an interesting week, and an educational one. I've learned that horses have eight times the number of nerve endings per square inch that people do; that Eli's exact weight is 1,254 pounds; that my entire frostbitten nose fits perfectly inside one of Eli's nostrils, and that if I wedge it in there and breathe really slowly, not only does it warm me up, it puts him in a state of sleepy euphoria right up until the moment when he sneezes all over me.

In short, I learned all sorts of fascinating things. What I did *not* learn, however, was the underlying cause of our troubles. The fact that the bone scan showed nothing significant is both good and bad. Good in that Eli has no measurable bone loss, or structural changes, or anything worthy of note; bad, in that if nothing's broken, there's nothing to fix, and therefore, no way to prevent this severe and puzzling lameness from reoccurring.

The orthopedic surgeon wants me to leave Eli barefoot for a month—no riding for *another* four weeks—to let his feet toughen up. I can put him out in a small paddock, provided the ground isn't rock hard, which, this being January, it *is*. As an alternative, I can let him run around on soft footing, but the internist who tested his lung function says he really could use more fresh air. But the ground is too hard to put him out with no shoes. I could try opening his window, but then the pipes are bound to freeze in the barn. So there you have it: there's the rock, there's the hard place, and there's Eli and me in between.

No one who's just spent three days and $3,000—including the hotel, rental car, trailer, and meals—to schlep a horse out of state in the worst weather of the year wants to be told by the top specialist in the area that her horse's case is a complete mystery. I could have heard that for a $45 barn fee from my local vet, which, come to think of it, I already have.

But even if I don't know how I'm going to keep my horse sound, there's something to be said for knowing definitively that Eli doesn't have any foot problems such as navicular disease, or a coffin bone fracture, or some other horrible condition that's likely to shorten his career or, more important, his life.

And there's a lot to be said for knowing that I can take this guy anywhere. I'm also happy to know that it isn't just me; that everyone who worked with him made it a point to tell me what a nice horse he is. The vet I liked best said it was obviously a result of the way that I've handled him.

Given the behavior of the horses around him, much of it not very good, I am awfully proud of my big sweet potato. All in all, I couldn't have asked him for more.

It's well after dark by the time we finally pull into the parking lot at Pegasus, unload Eli from Mike's trailer, and lead him back into the barn. Before I put him away for the night, I walk him into the indoor and turn him loose. He immediately drops to his knees and rolls on his back, again and again, grinding himself into the sweet dirt of home till the hospital smells are all gone.

* * *

FOR THE NEXT MONTH, my barefoot horse and I follow a simple routine: I arrive before dawn, feed him, groom him, and let him loose in the indoor. Now that I know nothing's seriously wrong, I'm a lot more relaxed about him running around.

I'm also more confident about my own judgment with regard to what I will or will not let him do. In that sense, the trip to Tufts was a watershed.

I look forward to these mornings of playing with Eli more than any that I can recall. The anxiety and dread that accompanied my lessons with Karen of late has finally lifted. I'm joyful again.

Prior to the bone scan, my relationship with my trainer had deteriorated to the point where I'd arrive at the barn with a lump in my throat and my stomach in knots. As soon as I sat on my horse's back, the tension passed seamlessly from my body to his.

I'd tried everything I could think of to make my relationship with Karen less toxic, but nothing seemed to work. In desperation, I'd bought us each a private session with a well-known sports psychologist, but our dynamic had failed to improve.

Our trainer-student relationship had become adversarial. By the time Tufts suggested I give Eli four weeks off to toughen his feet, I was so miserable and conflicted, the doctor's orders felt more like a blessing than a restriction.

I now have four blissful, unsupervised weeks to spend with my horse, doing whatever we damn well please. Four weeks to do whatever makes Eli and me happy. Four weeks to figure out why I'm paying someone good money to treat me like absolute crap.

* * *

THERE'S ANOTHER SIDE TO THE STORY, HOWEVER. I really like Karen, and I consider her a very good friend. Not in the ring—certainly not while she's tearing me apart—but the minute it's over, it's over.

I'll concede she's high maintenance. Our holiday lunch—conceived as a fun, festive outing—became a lengthy ordeal when she rejected one restaurant after another. When I finally suggested an upscale burger place, she acquiesced, only to reject that as well, after having seen the words "Black Angus" on the menu. They'd reminded her she was eating a steer.

Exasperating as she can be, she can also be fun. Funny, too. We have laughed like hyenas over breakfast, lunch, and dinner, and shared our darkest secrets time and again.

I have no idea what to do about her, so I do what I can, which is only hope that time will tell.

thirteen

APRIL 2000

Spring arrives early for a change. I'm nowhere near ready for ninety-degree weather in April, and neither is Eli. Still shaggy from the winter, he continues to be easily winded and to break a sweat without even trying.

With our four-week vacation over and his toughened-up feet in new shoes, it's time to get him moving again. I start by schooling him on a lunge line, indoors first, then out when the weather permits. He's a banshee in the beginning, as I've come to expect, but he soon settles down in the heat.

It feels strange to be sitting on him again after months of not riding, strange and not altogether good. At first, all I can think about is how high up I am, and how little strength I have relative to his. It's just starting to feel somewhat normal again when his attitude takes an irritable turn.

He flinches whenever I try to curry him. He pins his ears at the mounting block the minute I step into the stirrup, horse-speak for "leave me alone." One day he swishes his tail in annoyance as I swing my leg over his back. The next, he sidesteps away from the mounting block just as I'm getting on him, and I end up on my ass in the dirt.

I rule out the obvious: no apparent lameness, no back soreness, no fever, just overall crankiness and an unwillingness to work. Then the light bulb goes on in my head: Lyme disease. Of course! I summon the vet, who confirms it with a blood test.

Lyme disease, the scourge of the Northeast, is named for the Connecticut community where it was first detected in humans in 1975. A bacterial illness caused by the bite of infected deer ticks, Lyme is so prevalent in this part of the country it's a rare day when someone I know isn't being treated for it; if not the human, then her horse or her dog. Sometimes all three.

In infected horses, Lyme disease can cause stiffness and large-joint lameness, along with irritability and a bad attitude toward work. The good news is that it's highly treatable, especially in the early stages.

But despite being the treatment of choice for horses with Lyme, doxycycline only comes in one strength: 100 milligram tablets. This is fine for people, but one size does not fit all. And that is the bad news: For the next month or so, I must somehow get 100 tablets a day into my finicky, suspicious, irritable horse.

I try hiding his pills in sweet feed, the molasses-laced grain I dole out in small quantities for the same reason moms the world over learn to limit their children's intake of high-sugar cereals. I spend the better part of the next hour plucking damp, sticky orange tablets out of Eli's bedding.

"Frosting," says Mike.

I look at him dubiously. "Like, cake frosting? Surely not."

He nods emphatically. "Yup, they love it. Try strawberry."

So I do, and end up looking like I've just lost a food fight at a birthday party for five-year-old girls.

I hollow out a Granny Smith apple and stuff it with pills; Eli takes one whiff and turns on his haunches, presenting me with his backside.

I try hiding pills in doughnuts. Oatmeal cookies. Apple Jacks. Straight molasses. Maple syrup. Peppermints. Mashed bananas.

Finally, in desperation, I buy a coffee grinder and pulverize the pills into a powder. I then stir it into applesauce and plunge the whole mucky mess down his throat. *Homemade* applesauce at first, then store-bought when he makes it clear that as far as his taste buds are concerned, my grandmother's recipe has nothing on Mott's.

"Sorry, pal," I tell him. "But there is no good way to do this, so I'm afraid you're just going to have to cope."

He tries hiding his face in the corner when he sees me coming, dose syringe in hand, to no avail. Stretching his neck and pointing his chin at the ceiling proves far more effective. *Too* effective, since there's no way I can reach that high.

In the end, I cross tie him on the aisle and rely on the element of surprise to slide one hand under his halter to pull his lip up as I slip the loaded syringe through his bars, the gap between his incisors and molars, a technique I learned from Jackie years ago. This works fairly well right up until the day when it doesn't work at all anymore. It's hard to surprise a suspicious horse for thirty consecutive days.

Even though some days are a wash, in the end I manage to get more spiked applesauce into him than he manages to spit out all over me. Once again, my lovely lemon recovers.

SPRING 2001

After much agonizing, and a lot more list making, I decide to give Karen one last try. I do it because, as she keeps reminding me, she's the only decent trainer around. Because even though she can and does beat me up, she is kind to my horse. Because I very much want to be a better rider, and I don't know of another way to make that happen.

This time, I tell myself, I won't choke when my horse bolts, spooks, or spins. I won't curl up into a ball of defensive tension every time Karen raises her voice. This time I'll project an aura of self-confidence with both her and my horse. If I fake it long enough, maybe it will become real.

This time I'll also establish some limits in terms of what I'm willing to put up with from her. And if she exceeds them, I'll put a stop to this once and for all. No more second chances; I'll be done training with her for good.

Our inaugural lesson once Eli is sound comes off without a hitch. We are all three of us on our best behavior, and I come away feeling like this might just work.

Lesson number two is a total disaster. With a smirking Bonnie looking on, I'm right back to square one, and so is Karen. I can't do anything right; she can't stop screaming at me. What's more, I am furious, not even with her so much as myself. Why am I letting Bonnie throw me like this? Why can't I just forget that she's there?

After forty-five minutes bearing snarky witness to my humiliation, Bonnie turns and heads back toward the barn.

The minute her back is turned, I get my shit together pronto. With Karen standing there in silent, open-mouthed shock, I pick up the whip, shorten my reins, and do a remarkable impersonation of an upper-level dressage rider.

I can hear Karen in the center of the ring as we pass: "Oh, my God. *Holy shit!* OH MY GOD!"

Now we know. It's all there. It's all in me, every bit of everything I've ever learned from Jackie and Karen both. "That was the most amazing thing I've ever seen," Karen says wide-eyed, when I finally bring Eli to a halt. "That was *scary.*"

I nod, still angry. "I know how to do this. That's what makes it so hard. My body isn't the problem. It's my head that's the problem."

Karen grins. "Then we'll just have to have it removed."

˙ ⁎ ˙

ALL SUMMER, Karen takes it upon herself to try to aggravate me at every lesson in the hope I will once again transform anger into proficiency. Unfortunately, this approach mostly backfires, and we both end up angry as a result.

I'm at an impasse when the tragedy of September 11 occurs. In the seconds it takes for the towers to fall, the continent between me and my sister stretches into an infinite expanse. I wonder how long it will take to return to its normal traversable size, how long before people start getting on planes again, how long till I see her and her kids. I hug Mark especially hard that night, thankful to have been spared the loss of any of the people I love, mindful of those who have not.

With the world a changed place, along with my family and friends, I reach out for my four-legged lifesavers, the animals that help keep me grounded. Now more than ever, I find myself needing the comfort their familiar bulk provides. I redouble my efforts to stay in the moment when I'm walking the dog or riding my horse, given my heightened awareness that my time with them is limited and therefore precious.

*　*　*

AFTER THE HORRIFYING EVENTS of 9/11 that kept the world's attention riveted to the sky, I look forward to November's cathartic Leonid meteor shower as a kind of celestial cleansing.

The Leonids take place each November as Earth intercepts a trail of dust particles shed by comet Tempel-Tuttle on its orbit around the sun. Every thirty-two years, which is the length of the comet's orbit, the resulting meteor shower becomes a more prolific meteor storm, one that can last several years. This is the peak of the current storm. Instead of roughly fifty visible meteors an hour, there could be hundreds of thousands.

The best place to view this phenomenon is a secluded spot removed from city lights and the headlights of oncoming cars. I decide to get up at 3:00 AM and drive to the barn. If there's a better place to watch the night sky fill with shooting stars, I don't know where it could be.

Stopping for gas at the normally quiet twenty-four-hour convenience store midway between my house and the barn, I'm surprised to discover the joint is jumping. A party atmosphere prevails as everyone seems to be stocking up on sodas and snacks lest they starve to death while shooting-star gazing. God bless America.

I start seeing intense streaks of light shoot across the sky the minute I get on the highway. By the time I pull into the barn parking lot, I've seen dozens. The conditions are perfect: a clear sky with temperatures around 20°F. I kill the lights and shut off the car, and the sky over my head comes to life.

I'm seeing six or seven at a time, some so bright they leave vapor trails, a wondrous sight and an oddly moving one, made all the more meaningful, somehow, by my proximity to my sleeping horse. By the time the sun rises nearly two hours later, I've seen a lifetime's worth of shooting stars and felt a peace that's eluded me for some time.

Soothed by one of the great mysteries of the natural world, I wait till the last visible streak has made its journey across the brightening sky before turning my attention to another, heading inside to feed Eli his breakfast and begin a new day.

JANUARY 2002

Eli's right front suspensory ligament, the large elastic band that supports his weight and acts as a shock absorber in the lower leg, tears for the third time in five years the following winter. Among the most common—and recurring—injuries in equine athletes in general, and racehorses in particular, it's notoriously slow to heal because of the poor blood supply in the lower leg.

Icing, cold-hosing, hand-walking, and stall rest are the typical treatments. I also hire someone to give Eli daily laser treatments, as laser therapy has been proven to speed the healing process by stimulating greater blood flow to damaged tissues.

Once again, I am dealing with an injured, pent-up horse. Our modest twenty-minute walks don't even make a dent in Eli's energy level, and the invigorating cold weather, needless to say, doesn't help.

Every day that I manage to walk him around the indoor arena without incident, without him rearing or grabbing the lead rope, without him shaking his head, stamping his feet, or throwing a full-blown tantrum, is a good day. I cross them off on my calendar one by one, hoping upon hope that we'll get through this without further injury to either of us.

By March, the vet pronounces him 90 percent healed. I step up the walking and throw in a little grazing when the weather allows. Even though Eli is quick to blow up over the least little thing—a puff of wind, an empty gum wrapper, the orange construction cone that has mysteriously appeared on the front lawn—it's important for him to spend time outside getting some fresh air, and he's nowhere near ready to be turned loose in a paddock, not even a small one.

The better he feels, naturally, the fresher he becomes. Our little grazing sessions turn into a pitched battle of wills and reflexes: my will versus his reflexes. Determined not to let him reinjure himself, I enlist Mike's help, bribing him with large cups of coffee and breakfast pastries. Sweetheart that he is, he agrees not only to come outside with us but also to graze Eli for me on the days I can't get there.

Like the bratty child who morphs into a perfect angel the minute Daddy comes home, Eli is smart enough not to act up in Mike's presence. Whenever he accompanies us to the front lawn, my gelding is as calm as a plow horse. Mike talks me into removing the chain across Eli's nose, my only leverage when he misbehaves, because naturally, with Mike at our side, we no longer need it. He then demonstrates the Mike Method of establishing dominance.

"See how I'm not letting him drop his head to eat?"

I see.

"I'm saying no, you can't graze there. I'll show you when and where you can graze."

As Mike crisscrosses the lawn with Eli in tow, my horse makes no attempt whatsoever to lower his head to eat grass; instead, he minces along as politely as a Westminster poodle until Mike finally stops and "invites" him to drop his head and eat. Eli accepts the invitation without budging from the radius allowed by the lead rope, as opposed to dragging the human at the other end of it all over the lawn the way he usually does with me.

"See? Nothing to it," Mike says triumphantly.

"Yeah, sure. A little testosterone and he's a model of decorum."

"C'mere. You try it."

I dutifully take the lead rope from Mike's hand and swap places with him. Eli, frantically scarfing the grass, doesn't appear to notice that there's been a shift change. I thank Mike for the tutorial and he heads back inside, whereupon Eli lifts his head, sees the construction cone, and freaks.

By the time I half drag him back inside the barn, Mike is nowhere to be found and I am at my wit's end. I forcibly return Eli to his stall, write Mike a note, and drive home muttering like a crazy woman.

Two days later, I arrive at the barn to find a photo taped to the front of Eli's door. The picture shows him serenely grazing away on the lawn, the orange construction cone neatly balanced on his rump.

THE FOLLOWING MONTH, with Eli finally in the home stretch of his protracted recovery, I'm determined not to let anything impede his progress. Our last hurdle, a friend's wedding in Philadelphia, looms large on the calendar. It's a night wedding a three-hour drive from our house, which means we'll have to stay overnight.

I'm relieved when Missy offers to handle Eli's routine for that weekend. An experienced horsewoman, she also knows Eli and Eli knows her. And I know he will be in good hands. To quell the last of my anxiety, I make exhaustive lists of instructions, not unlike the ones my friend Claire made when she and her husband went away for the weekend, leaving their two-year-old daughter, Ellie, with a neighbor. I'll never forget the sight of Ellie running naked down Hickory Lane, having let herself out without anyone noticing. Lists are not foolproof.

Still, more for my sake than Missy's, I write down my instructions. I caution her against taking Eli outside if it's windy or cold, or if there are significant numbers of kids and ponies out on the lawn. She should feel free to just walk him indoors; by all means, she should put the chain over his nose. If he misbehaves, she shouldn't worry about walking him at all, just put him on cross ties, groom him, and feed him some treats. The most important thing is for neither of them to get hurt.

If, on the other hand, she *should* deem it safe to take him outside for some grass, she should be sure to keep him away from the road. Keep the chain over his nose and both eyes trained on him at all times. Because she often brings her two Vizslas with her to the barn, I also remind her that Eli is skittish around dogs, particularly when they run up behind him, as has happened more than once on the trail.

Missy laughs at my lists, and I apologize for my obsessive-compulsive behavior. "Normally, I wouldn't be so uptight about being gone, but he's right on the cusp of being able to go back to work, and I'm a little superstitious about being away from him when he's this close."

Missy nods knowingly. "Perfectly understandable, Nance. Don't worry. You just go and enjoy yourself. Everything here will be fine."

On the day before we're due to leave, I bring bags and bags of carrots to the barn for Missy to share between Eli and Giovanni, her horse. I go over the rules one last time with her, stressing safety above all else. The forecast calls for a cold, gusty Saturday, hardly ideal for a horse that's been cooped up for months. "Remember, it won't kill him to stay in for a day or two, so please feel free not to take him outside."

By the time Mark and I hit the road the next day, I'm finally ready to let go of my fears. I've done everything I can think of to ensure Eli's and Missy's safety. There's nothing left to do but to relax and have a good time.

We first drive to Mark's brother's house in a suburb of Philadelphia, where we'll be spending the night. We arrive with just enough time to say a quick hello and change into our good clothes for the drive into the city.

I'm putting on makeup in the bathroom when my sister-in-law, Donna, knocks on the door. "You have a phone call from the barn," she says, handing me the receiver. My stomach turns over; this can't be good.

"Hello?"

"This is Becky? At Pegasus?" I recognize the name of one of the kids who helps feed on the weekends.

"What's wrong, Becky?"

"Well, your horse kicked Missy and now he's, like, loose. What do you want me to do?"

"WHAT? WHAT DO YOU MEAN, HE KICKED MISSY? WHERE IS SHE?"

"Um, she left? In the ambulance."

I feel nauseous. "How bad is she hurt?"

"I'm not sure. What do you want me to do about Eli?"

"Oh, I don't know. Why don't you throw some grain in a bucket and GO CATCH HIM BEFORE HE KILLS SOMEONE?"

Silence.

"GO! NOW! I'LL CALL YOU BACK IN A FEW MINUTES."

With shaking hands I punch in Karen's number. She answers, thank God, on the first ring. "The barn just called. Eli kicked Missy and she was taken away in an ambulance, and I'm on my way to Philadelphia. Could you do me a huge favor and go to the hospital and find out what the hell's going on?"

"On my way." Just like that. That's the thing about Karen. The woman knows how to take charge.

From the car on our way to the ceremony I call the barn back and get Eva, one of the other trainers. "Oh, Eli's fine," she says in her most blasé tone, the one she reserves for catastrophic events.

Having run into an empty paddock, Eli has been captured and is now in his stall, though not without having run himself ragged. Eva says he looks "a little off," which probably means he's three-legged lame. She has no information about Missy, having been out to lunch when the incident occurred, so I ask her to cold-hose and wrap Eli's legs. I then hang up to await Karen's report from the hospital.

Midway across the Ben Franklin Bridge, I'm struck by how oddly familiar it feels to be piecing together snippets of bad news from multiple sources in several locations. I feel like I'm back at The Associated Press.

The wedding is lovely, what I see of it, anyway. I'm back and forth between the reception and the hallway outside, which I keep dashing into with Mark's cell phone to try to connect with Karen. When she finally answers, she tells me that Missy has a couple of broken ribs but otherwise seems okay. "Did she tell you what happened?"

"Yeah. She said he kicked her."

"I know, but *why?* What else was going on?"

"Nothing."

"You mean he just up and kicked her for no good reason?"

"That's what she says."

Hmmm. "Well, if that's the case, he's obviously in a lot of trouble."

Just the opening Karen was hoping for. "You've got to stop overtreating him. He's gotten way too spoiled. You need to go a week without giving him anything. Not a single thing."

A week? A *week?* Was that even possible?

"Okay, tell Missy I'll come by Monday to see her. And tell her I'll groom and graze Giovanni till she's better. Thanks for stepping in. I really appreciate it."

We hang up and I return to the party, but for the rest of the night and all the next day, I ruminate over what I've been told. It's hard for me to imagine Eli kicking Missy without provocation. My horse may be spoiled, but he isn't mean.

Still, I go up to the barn Monday morning and read Eli the riot act. I tell him he hurt someone and that he has to be punished for it. No treats for a week. The minute he starts pawing the floor, I give him a smack so resounding it stings my hand. He looks at me, stunned. I am clearly not the person he has come to know and expect. The loving, besotted human carrot dispenser has been replaced by a doppelgänger. *Be afraid.*

Judging from the smirks on their faces, the muckers are clearly amused by the little show I'm putting on. "Big boy's in trouble, eh? Heh heh heh," one of them chortles. I ignore him and lead Eli into the ring.

There I pick up a lunge whip and crack it. "TROT." He trots. But he's so gimpy on his ailing right front, I have to stop him. "Nice going," I grumble. "And you were practically all healed."

I put him back in his stall and cross the indoor to the stalls on the opposite side, where I proceed to take Giovanni out and groom him, then lavish him with all the affection and treats I withheld from Eli. After a half-hour grazing session, I put him back inside and go shopping for a get-well basket for Missy. I buy her flowers and food, magazines and bath salts. I then drive to her house, where her taciturn husband lets me in without so much as a hello and goes to fetch her.

I don't think it's possible for me to feel any worse till I watch her shuffle painfully across the living room and try to ease into a chair.

"Oh, God, Missy, I'm so sorry," I murmur.

"The thing is, Nance, he did it on purpose."

"What do you mean?"

"I mean he looked me right in the eye and then nailed me."

Wait a minute. My horse? The hell he did. "Tell me what happened."

"I just did."

"Back up a minute," I say. "Tell me from the beginning. Where were you when he kicked you?"

"I was getting something out of my trailer."

"So you were outside? Near the road? Where was he?"

"I had him on a long line. I'd just gone in the trailer to get something."

"Was anyone else there?"

Missy paused to shift her weight in her chair, wincing. "A woman in a car stopped to ask directions, so I was telling her—"

I hold up my hand. "Whoa. Hold on a second. So you've got Eli on a lead line, you're inside your trailer and you're giving some woman directions."

"Right."

I immediately begin channeling my inner lawyer: *Wouldn't that make it a little tough for him to look you in the eye?*

"Okay," I say. "Go on."

"I came back out of the trailer. Then the dogs ran up."

"They ran up behind Eli?"

"Yeah."

"And that's when he looked you in the eye and kicked you on purpose for no good reason?"

Silence.

"Missy, I'm *really, really* sorry Eli kicked you and I feel *terrible* that you got hurt. But you can't tell me he did it on purpose."

"Well, I——"

I cut her off in mid-excuse. "Hear me out. I gave you those instructions for a reason." I proceed to tick them off on my fingers. "One: Don't take him outside if it's windy. Two: Put a chain over his nose. Three: If you do go outside, don't go near the road. Four: Don't take your eyes off him for a minute. Five: He's afraid of your dogs."

Missy finally looks sheepish. "I guess it wasn't entirely his fault," she says, hanging her head.

"Please know this: He is not off the hook. I will hold his hooves to the fire for the next seven days. No treats, no grass, no nothing. He will know there are consequences for his behavior. But I also want you to tell Karen exactly what you just told me because I don't want her thinking he did this without provocation. Will you do that?"

She nods.

"Okay, thanks. Please take good care of yourself and I'll take care of Giovanni for you in the meantime. Call me if there's anything you need."

I give her a kiss on the top of her head and let myself out. For the next week, I become Eli's marine. I make good on my promise to withhold all treats, and by the end of his unofficial boot camp, his manners are impeccable. I proudly mention this to Karen when I run into her outside Giovanni's stall, and she looks at me, aghast.

"A *week?* An entire *week?*"

"Seven days."

"Not even a carrot?"

I shake my head. "Nope."

"Well, for God's sake, go *give* him something already! Jeez! The poor horse!"

I shake my head at her in exasperation and hurry back across the indoor to Eli, a bunch of Giovanni's carrots under my arm.

* * *

OVER THE NEXT SEVERAL WEEKS, I help groom and graze Giovanni as promised. I wait about a month, until Missy feels stronger, before bringing up unfinished business.

"How would you feel about stopping by to see Eli," I ask her one morning while we watch Karen school Giovanni.

Missy bites her lip. "I don't know."

"Well, think about it, please. I don't want this to become a big rift between you. You and Eli have known each other a long time."

Missy sighs. "You're right, we have."

"And he's more than paid his debt to society." I remind her of the week he'd endured without treats. "He didn't do it on purpose," I add. "There was too much going on that day, more than he could handle, and he reverted to type. He is a horse, after all. But you guys really need to make up. Come on. I'll go with you."

Missy nods slowly, one arm still wrapped protectively around her rib cage. "Okay, let's go."

Together we cross the indoor to Eli's side of the barn, where we find him eating hay in his stall. "Hey, look who's here to see you," I call. Eli pops his head up, takes one look at Missy, and flees to the back of his stall, with his head in the corner and his butt facing us.

"See that?" I say to Missy. "That's how bad he feels."

I reach into my pocket for some molasses cookies and hand them to my injured friend. "Go."

"Hey there, Eli," she says, as she opens the door and goes in.

⋆

AN OLD FRIEND RESURFACES from out of the blue, a college buddy with whom I'd lost touch. After thirty-odd years without contact, we discover we're less than an hour apart.

I invite her over to catch up on our lives. Hers has taken a remarkable twist. After college, she joined the military service—less out of patriotism than an unrelenting appetite for cocaine. Because she couldn't afford rehab, she opted to enlist. She'd gone cold turkey during basic training and thereafter had enjoyed a long and successful military career.

I couldn't have been more shocked had she told me she'd become a cannibal, but her ingenuity impresses me, to say nothing of her discipline. It also gives me an idea.

If I were in better shape, I'd undoubtedly be a better rider: stronger, more athletic, better able to gut out an entire ride without having to take a break, something Karen doled out grudgingly.

So I sign up to work out at a local gym three times a week with a retired marine. Given that his idea of fun is running the bleachers at ball fields, I go in poised for the worst, but our initial sessions are more diagnostic than debilitating. His first order of business is to determine my level of fitness. He assures me the demoralizing stuff will come later.

At Session Five he tosses me a twelve-pound medicine ball I'm to throw backward over my head at a wall. I must then squat and grab it as it comes off the wall and rolls back to me between my legs. I'm to do this as fast as I can—one continuous motion—while he operates the stopwatch.

Toward the end of the first set, the blood starts rushing to my head as I squat down to grab for the ball, to the point where I nearly fall over. People on either side stop exercising to watch as the marine barks my orders at me: "Thirty seconds, COME ON, fifteen seconds, LET'S GO, GO, GO! COME ON! We're gonna work this flab right off you!"

So I do. I COME ON. I GO, GO, GO, and when it's finally over, we do several more medicine ball things, then some elastic band things, things that are like rowing, things that are like ski jumping, things that make me *wish* I were rowing and ski jumping.

When it finally ends with "*Good job! Bye-bye,*" I head for my car keys on the pegboard near the door and start to worry about how I am going to negotiate the little step down from the curb.

My legs are shaking and my quads feel like the knots of bark on a tree. I lower myself into the car mostly using my arms, then drive home and reverse the process. I have trouble negotiating the three little steps to my front door.

The cramping has only just begun as I sit at the table to wait for the sweat to dry and the shaking to stop. My legs haven't hurt like this in twenty years, not since a White Mountain bike trip with Mark that began with a five-mile climb and ended thirty miles later when I beached myself on a traffic island.

Mark returns home from taking himself out to lunch and sees me sitting there with my scarlet face and bulging quads, and I can tell right away he's not going to ask how it went, how I feel, or anything else that might give me a soupçon of satisfaction.

So I tell him anyway. He has no comment. For an instant, I want a divorce even more than I want a shower.

That night, I go to bed early, desperate for some relief, and find I can no longer lie on my stomach; I can't take the pressure on my legs. Getting from the bed to the bathroom the next morning is a hobbling, furniture-clutching experience. Lowering myself on the toilet makes me wish I'd just wet the damn bed. And on it goes throughout the day till I show up at Amy's for a potluck dinner with a tub of my best lobster salad.

Finally, an attentive, appreciative audience! I could kiss her. Then Katie joins us and I get to tell it all again. Curled up in her chair, drinking wine and smoking a cigarette, Katie listens in horrified silence, then asks why in God's name I am doing this to myself.

We talk. We drink. We laugh. Amy fetches me three Advils and a couple of Ambiens for later. These are good— *very* good—friends. Finally, though, the pain's getting to me and I struggle to my feet to head home. I thank them, say good night and step off Amy's porch, taking a header onto her gravel driveway and spilling leftover lobster salad into my purse.

The next day, I return from seeing Eli—"seeing" being all that I can physically do—to a message from Katie: "Though I applaud what you're doing, I think you've let this guy push you to extremes that are well beyond what you should be doing, and I'm just calling to see how the heck you're doing 'cause I've rarely seen anyone in so much pain. (Heavy sigh.) Okay, baby, I'm just checking on ya. Lotsa love."

I smile and am about to listen to her message again when I realize something's missing. I climb the stairs, not quite as painfully as before, and head for my office, where I scan the shelves for the sign I swiped from Pegasus: TAKE

YOUR PAIN IN SILENCE. I carry it back down, drag a chair over to the answering machine, and lower myself into it. I close my eyes, put my feet up, and hit replay, listening to the soothing sound of Katie's voice again and again.

That night I fall in the yard while attempting to pick up some dog poop. I lean over, get dizzy, am unable to squat, lose my balance, and career around, bouncing off the drainpipe and landing with my hip on the threshold of the door to the back porch.

At the barn, I have a field day with my big purple bruise, showing it off to anyone who will look. I take a photo of it and e-mail it to my sister, my mother, my niece. Their horror cheers me up and takes my mind off my quads. Riding is out of the question. Instead, I work Eli from the ground.

I'm just beginning to walk normally when it's time for my next session. I tell the marine that he needs to take it easy on me, that my quads are off the menu for the day. He looks at me in mock surprise and says, "We train your whole body! We don't do piecemeal." I explain about the muscle spasms, the stairs, and the falls, but nothing gets through. So I do what I promised myself I wouldn't do: I drop 'em and show him my bruise.

Whereupon the marine shrugs. He then says, "I've had worse."

So I do the *other* thing I vowed never to do: I blubber. A big mistake. Huge. He begins lecturing me in the most patronizing manner imaginable. *"Do you remember what your goals are?"* Yes. *"Do you remember what you asked me to help you do?"* Yes. My lip is quivering, my eyes tearing up.

Then he tells me a little story that makes me want to kill him again and again, preferably for the rest of my life; a story about a caterpillar and a butterfly. "Did you know that parts of the caterpillar actually die before it emerges as a butterfly?" I look at him dubiously through unshed tears.

"You can look it up," he says. "It's the truth."

Caterpillars are soft-bodied and slow moving. Perfect. Although this workout leaves me barely able to lift my arms high enough to transport my hands to my computer keyboard, I do look it up. And here's what I find: "Many observations have indicated that *cell death* plays a considerable role during physiological processes of multicellular organisms, particularly during *embryogenesis* and metamorphosis."

So he's right. Parts of me *will* die, which might explain why I'm having difficulty taking my pulse.

At Session Seven we move on to free weights. Mark is here, too, working out on his own, and the marine asks to meet him. I lead him over to my husband, who is doing some impressive lifting and sweating, and they engage in some good-natured banter at guess who's expense.

"You've been killing my wife," Mark says.

"It's what I do." Ha, ha, ha!

Then the marine goes away for a week, and I celebrate by sucking down Cosmopolitans with Katie, Amy, and Claire, and proving for the umpty-umpth time that left to my own devices, I have an unfortunate tendency to be sedentary.

But that weekend, when I do finally ride my horse, I feel downright bionic. I work Eli for an hour without a break. By the time I'm done, he is sweaty and blowing. I am neither. And I owe it all to the US Marines.

Now, if only mine would stop calling me "Cupcake."

₊

BOLSTERED BY MY NEWFOUND STRENGTH, I finally part ways with Karen. Even though it's been a long time coming, it only now feels like the right choice to me. Although Karen is no longer the right trainer for Eli and me, I will always be grateful to her for having seen the good in him right from the start. When I look back on our years together, I will endeavor to do the same for her.

fourteen

MAY 2004

*T*RUTH BE TOLD, Pegasus is a bit of a dump. Stained tiles dangle from the falling bathroom ceiling and giant pink tongues of insulation loll from the walls. Condensation drips from the skylights on warm winter mornings and falls as a steady rain on our heads.

But somehow, none of that detracts from the way I feel about the place. I love it here. I don't ever want to leave.

And though, technically speaking, Pegasus has been for sale since long before Eli and I arrived, I never thought Mike would actually sell it. Perhaps more to the point, I never thought anyone would actually *buy* it.

I turn out to be wrong on both counts.

In retrospect, of course, I should've seen this coming. Mike has been divesting himself of his responsibilities for the boarding operation for some time, having leased the stalls on our side of the barn to Eva, a trainer. I've been writing my board checks to her for months now.

Clearly, I've been in denial.

We get our first look at the new owner just as the first buds of spring are starting to swell on the trees. His plans call for major reconstruction, along with a whopping board increase. It's pretty obvious that by the time he's done remodeling the place, none of the current boarders, me included, will be able to afford to stay here.

Construction begins even before we've had a chance to scout around for a new barn. Most mornings, I arrive to the sound of drilling as workmen dismantle stalls on all sides.

Eva is checking out barns for lease in the area and re-cruiting candidates to move with her. I have some mis-givings. Although she's pleasant enough, I find myself trusting her less and less as time goes on. Stories have got-ten back to me about her doing things I've expressly told her not to, such as allowing Greta, Eli's young groupie, to take him out of his stall to groom. But because I have no other option, against my better judgment I agree to give Eva a chance.

The weekend before we're due to move, I lead Eli out-side for one last grazing session on the front lawn, one of a number of features we're both going to miss.

It's Derby Day, the first Saturday in May, and I'm feeling nostalgic. As a young reporter, I covered two Kentucky Derbies. I got soused on mint juleps, steamed down the Ohio River on the paddlewheel *Delta Queen*, and watched the sun rise over the back side of Churchill Downs with AP's legendary horse-racing writer, Ed Schuyler Jr., who earned his nickname, "Fast Eddie," by dictating stories al-most as fast as the races were run.

All of that seems like a long time ago now as I stand grazing my not-quite-fast-enough racehorse under a powder-blue sky on this balmy spring morning. As is my custom, I say a silent prayer for a safe race for all the Thoroughbreds about to be put to the test in the mile-and-a-quarter proving ground in Louisville. The air is soft and warm, and for the first time in weeks, the construction crew dismantling Pegasus is noticeably absent. It's finally quiet enough to hear the birds sing.

Watching Eli tear up the tender spring grass, I reflect on how far he has come in the six years that I've owned him. Another of his suspensory injuries has all but healed without incident, and he finally seems to have settled down and matured.

I can look back on a number of incidents in which he proved himself more than trustworthy: the time we were cantering a tight circle around a jump and got too close to it. I whacked the standard with my foot, losing not only my stirrup but my balance; Eli, feeling my sudden loss of equilibrium, saved me by stopping dead in his tracks.

I returned the favor the day he was nosing around by the heavy spectators' bench in the front corner of the indoor and inadvertently hooked his reins around its iron arm. Before I could reach over to unhook him, he panicked and flew backward into the center of the ring, dragging the weighty bench along with him. By talking to him calmly, I was able to get him to stop long enough for me to free him. Although it took several minutes for him to regain his composure, he then let me lead him right back to the bench to reassure him it posed no further danger. He learned to keep a respectful distance from that iron arm, and he was never frightened by it again.

There've been other incidents, too—when he got a lunge line wrapped around one of his legs; when he ripped a leg strap and got tangled in his blanket; when a quarter-sheet slipped out from under his saddle, causing the saddle to slide off his back and under his belly.

And on and on, through one potentially disastrous situation after another, he and I have learned to watch out for each other. I'm about to commend him on this, when for reasons unknown—a flashback, perhaps, to his brief sojourn at the track—he suddenly pops his head up, snorts once, and takes off as if shot from a cannon as I stand there foolishly holding the other end of the leash.

Judging by the speed of his departure, I know right away there'll be no stopping him. All I can do is watch helplessly as the thirty-foot line unfurls in my hand. But lest he undo five long months of stall rest, I stubbornly try to hold on. Big mistake. He wrenches the rubber donut at the end of the line from my hand and disappears around the back of the barn, trailing the lunge line behind him.

Then I'm screaming for help: "LOOSE HORSE!!" Two of the muckers and one of Eva's assistants come running. I needn't have panicked. Eli's easy enough to capture—he has speed but no stamina—and as I drag him back into the barn, I'm too busy lecturing him to notice anything aside from how angry I feel. I wrap his legs as a preventive measure and throw him back into his stall.

Only then do I slowly become aware of an odd sensation in my left hand. I pull off my glove and discover that my left pinky is now fingerprint side up. A sudden wave of nausea hits me, and I sit down hard on one of the bales of hay stacked on the aisle.

Just as I do, Eva sticks her head out of the tack room and looks at me questioningly. I hold up my hand and she says, as I knew she would, "I've seen worse." I also know what comes next: Frozen peas.

Frozen peas are Eva's treatment of choice for everything from compound fractures to the common cold. Once again, she does not disappoint. She sashays down the aisle to the refrigerator in the office and returns with the Jolly Green Giant.

"Here," she says in her most world-weary tone. "Put this on it. You'll be fine."

Although I'm reasonably sure I need medical attention, I comply. Actually, the frozen peas don't feel half bad. My finger is beginning to throb.

"Thanks, but I think maybe I'd better go to the emergency room. My finger's bent sideways and it's facing the wrong way. Frozen peas aren't going to fix that."

Eva ponders that a moment, as if building a case to the contrary. Then: "There's a walk-in clinic just down the road," she says. "But I don't think they open till 10:00."

I look at my watch: 9:15.

"You know what? I think I'll head over there just in case there's a line."

There is. Half the town appears to have crammed itself into the waiting room. I'm surrounded by coughing, runny-nosed children. Surely a dislocated finger trumps a head cold. I go up to the front desk waving my injured paw. "This really, really hurts. How long a wait do I have?"

The receptionist takes my insurance card and hands me a clipboard with *War and Peace* attached. "Fill out these forms," she says without looking up. "We'll get you in as soon as we can."

Nearly two hours later, a harried-looking nurse finally ushers me into an examining room and hands me a gown. "Put this on. The doctor will be right with you."

I throw the gown on a chair, muttering "It's my *finger*, you idiot," and wait another fifteen minutes without seeing a soul. Finally, an even more harried-looking man in a white coat arrives, takes one look at my finger and says, "Oh, wow. We can't treat that here. You need to go to a hospital."

"The only place I'm going is postal," I say through gritted teeth. "I've been sitting here since 9:30. I refuse to go sit in some emergency room for another four hours. Just fix it. You're a doctor. How hard can it be?"

He backs out of the room shaking his head at me, whereupon I finally burst into tears. I'm about to call Mark when an angel knocks on the door frame and enters. "I'm a nurse-practitioner," she says, "not a doctor. And I've never done this before. But I used to work for an orthopedic practice and I've seen it done many times. Do you want me to take a stab at it?"

"Yes," I say. "Please. Do it."

She injects my hand with a numbing agent and waits for it to take effect. I'm only vaguely aware of a tugging sensation. Then I hear her say, "Okay, it's done."

"You're kidding!" I look down at my hand and though my left pinkie is badly swollen and my knuckle is twice its normal size, I'm relieved to be looking at fingernail instead of fingerprint.

"You fixed it! Thank you so much! I really appreciate it."

"Glad I could help." She writes me a prescription for Percocet, instructs me to see my own doctor first thing Monday morning, and sends me on my way.

Back home finally, by midafternoon, I beg off on dinner with my in-laws. Instead, I swallow my Percocet and pass out on the living room couch with the TV tuned in to the Derby and my devoted Nurse Jake on the floor next to me. After several hours of pre-race buildup, the favorite, Smarty Jones, overtakes the pacesetter, Lion Heart, with a furlong to go, becoming the first unbeaten Derby winner since Seattle Slew in 1977. I manage to sleep through the whole thing.

The hand surgeon my doctor refers me to says there's nothing to be done about my pinkie. My proximal interphalangeal joint—the middle knuckle, in layman's terms—will forever stick up like a pup tent, a souvenir of that beautiful Derby Day.

* * *

IN MY PREVIOUS LIFE as an AP feature writer, I took full advantage of my editor's love of animals to secure myself a front-row seat at events the average horse enthusiast never gets to see. In addition to the two Kentucky Derbies I helped cover, I also attended the annual yearling sale in Lexington, Kentucky, at which a bay colt known only as No. 215 sold for a world record $13.1 million.

On another assignment in the Bluegrass Region of Kentucky, I spent a day in the breeding shed at Claiborne Farm where the late Secretariat bestowed his favors. The sight of Big Red prancing down the bridle path for his date with an eagerly awaiting filly is the sort of thing a horse lover never forgets.

I watched Seattle Slew, the world's only undefeated Triple Crown winner, out for his morning gallop around Slew Downs, his own private one-eighth-mile track at the venerable Spendthrift Farm. Born with a crooked front leg, Slew sold as a yearling for $17,500 and went on to become one of the biggest bargains in horse-racing history, with an estimated value that represented a return on his owners' investment of 521,093 percent. He won $1.2 million on the track before moving on to the breeding shed. There, he sired more than a hundred stakes winners and ignited the dreams of rookie investors everywhere before dying in his sleep at the relatively ripe age of twenty-eight on May 7, 2002, the twenty-fifth anniversary of his 1977 Kentucky Derby win.

Before True Tone became Eli, my horse had a previous life, too, one that I know little about. He did come with some baggage, however. Along with the faded tattoo on the inside of his upper lip and his unfortunate tendency to crib, his frequent episodes of lameness may have been a legacy from his early training, however brief, as a racehorse, when he most likely was asked to run short distances at high speeds.

Because he also came with something else—his original name—I'm able to piece together a few little scraps of his past with records from the Jockey Club, the breed registry for all Thoroughbreds foaled in North America.

All of today's Thoroughbreds, mine included, can trace their paternal lineage back to one of three stallions brought to Europe between the late seventeenth and early eighteenth centuries to engender a breed of champions. As history records, they were the Darley Arabian, the fastest horse in Syria; the Byerly Turk, a war hero; and the Godolphin Arabian, discovered, as legend has it, pulling a peasant's cart in Paris.

These three foundation sires were bred to stronger but less exceptional local mares to create a new breed of horse, one that could carry weight swiftly over longer distances.

All Thoroughbreds share a universal birthday. On January 1, New Year's Day, they officially turn a year older. By typing in Eli's unfortunate racing name, True Tone, and the year he was foaled, 1990, I'm able to find the actual date and location of his birth: April 17 in New York state. But the only other detail about him that the Jockey Club considers worthy of note is summed up in a single pejorative word: "Unraced."

In the past, whenever I've attempted to find out more about Eli's early life, the official trail has always ended there. Not surprising, since a gelded Thoroughbred with no racing record would seem to be of little interest to an organization "dedicated to the improvement of Thoroughbred breeding and racing."

This time, however, because of a promotional offer, I'm able to call up Eli's five-generation pedigree. And that's where things start to get interesting: I recognize the names of several of his relatives, most notably his great-grandfather, Northern Dancer; his great-*great*-grandfather, Gallant Man; and his great-great-*great*-grandfathers, the most accomplished of all: Count Fleet and Native Dancer, ranked fifth and seventh, respectively, on *The Blood-Horse*'s list of the Top 100 Racehorses of the Twentieth Century.

Well, now. It seems my horse is descended from racing royalty. I feel a shameless bout of braggadocio coming on.

Before I have much chance to crow about Eli's blue-bloodlines, however, I come upon this humbling statistic:

It seems 75 percent of US Thoroughbreds can be traced back to Native Dancer. It would appear Native Dancer got around.

Whether his disproportionate influence over the Sport of Kings has been a good thing or a bad thing seems to depend on who's talking. Either way, the benefits of genetic diversity tend to be undervalued in a sport in which speed counts for everything. And sooner or later, a shrinking gene pool brings familial flaws into sharp relief. Native Dancer's line is no exception, as evidenced by Barbaro, the 2006 Derby winner that fractured three bones in his right hind in the Preakness Stakes, an injury that ultimately led to his death.

Bad feet apparently run in the family.

A few words, though, about those feet, courtesy of The Jockey Club: "Thoroughbreds are also equipped with the most athletic feet in the world: hooves. The Thoroughbred's unique foot structure gives it built-in cushioning to withstand the equivalent of 100 times the force of gravity on each hoof, which is the force exerted when a Thoroughbred is running at full speed."

There is a saying in the horse world: No hoof, no horse. A lame horse can neither work nor play, which is why good farriers are worth their weight in gold. Eli and I have had the good fortune to have known three such highly skilled artists over the years. Without them, my horse would never have lasted this long.

Our current shoer, Mark Reilly, is a former rodeo cowboy who sometimes listens to classical music as he pounds nails into horses' hooves. A plainspoken son of the landlocked Midwest, he captains his own sailboat on weekends, and once sent his regrets to a barn party I was hosting because it happened to be the same weekend the rodeo cowboy was jetting off to Napa Valley to dine at The French Laundry. Only in Fairfield County.

Another unsung yet irreplaceable member of Team Eli is our remarkable chiropractor-acupuncturist, who visits twice a year to help keep him pain free. A former conventional equine practitioner, Rosemary Ganser pursued training and certification in veterinary acupuncture and chiropractic after seeing it work on a horse that had been medically treated unsuccessfully for recurring intestinal impaction.

I'll never forget the first time this slender, attractive woman treated Eli, working her way along his body with such precision and finesse, he sighed with relief and pleasure. He then turned his head to look at her as if to memorize her features and say thanks. Time and again, with nothing but her bare hands and estimable skill, she has alleviated pain, detected underlying medical problems, and restored flexibility in my aging gelding. We both look forward to her too-infrequent visits.

⋆

THE BARN EVA FINDS for us is dirty and dark, with low ceilings and barred windows, the smaller, older, poorer stepchild of two barns that make up the property. A mistake from the very beginning, and an omen of worse things to come.

Jake, my steadfast companion and muddy-nosed silly boy, leaves his Sunday dinner uneaten and succumbs to liver cancer within the week, taking with him a piece of my heart.

Without a trainer, I all but stop riding. Eli, cooped up in the dark barn and perpetually covered with hives, becomes withdrawn and depressed. As do I—too withdrawn and depressed to do what I know I should: go out and find him a better place to live. For the first time since I've owned him, I feel like a bad mother.

Even though I continue to visit him four days a week, I dislike the barn so much that once there, I seldom stay very long. As a result, I'm spending less time with Eli, and our relationship starts to suffer. In lieu of affection, I get indifference; he withholds his nickered greeting and pins his ears at me when I go to return him to his stall.

We end up staying a little over a year, far too long. I regret every minute of it.

⋆

AUGUST 2005

With all-day turnout, an owner who lives on the premises, and a roomy corner stall with big windows on two sides, Dragonfly Farm, Eli's new home, has a lot to recommend it. The lack of amenities, however, will take a little getting used to.

There's no wash stall or hot water for horses' showers, just a hose attached to a spigot outside. Nor is there a proper bathroom for humans. There's only an outhouse, a rather drafty one at that.

The indoor arena, in a separate building from our barn, is on the small side, and the footing seems skimpy and hard-packed. The outdoor ring, though good-sized, tends to flood in wet weather; the dirt paddocks turn to mud when it rains.

Even so, I think we'll be happy here. There are cushier places, to be sure, but I've heard too many horror stories about show barns with all the bells and whistles—manicured grounds, heated lounges, laundry facilities, tack shops, and so forth—owned by people who may love horses but who seem to know very little about their care. And I've seen too many horse owners seduced by luxurious trappings and sucked into bad situations that begin with exorbitant board bills and end with their horses getting hurt.

I've been at this for a while now, and it's time to start trusting my gut. My instincts tell me that Eli will be safe here, and that it's the right place for us to strengthen our bond after our brief but unhappy tenure at Eva's.

The owner, a woman named Beth who's exactly my age, strikes me as honest and hardworking, and the horses that live here seem calm and well cared for. Eli adjusts in record time to this relatively quiet, tranquil farm where the lack of drama suits both of us fine.

In some ways, Dragonfly is a bit of a hardscrabble place, utilitarian and spare. In that sense, it resembles its owner. Beth is petite and wiry, with close-cropped brown hair just beginning to gray and solemn eyes behind wire-rimmed glasses. She came here as a boarder and bought the place when the previous owner decided to move away.

I'm relieved to be dealing with someone as no-nonsense and straightforward as Beth. So what if there's an outhouse instead of a bathroom? In exchange for her plainspoken, no-bullshit ways, I'd pee in a litter box.

Over coffee in Beth's kitchen, I fill her in on Eli's previous exploits, his rather extensive medical history, and his proclivity for disasters large and small. Although she's too polite to openly roll her eyes at Nancy, the Neurotic New Boarder, I get the distinct impression she's rolling them inwardly. I can't help but chuckle to myself, given what she must be thinking. Knowing Eli, it's only a matter of time before she sees for herself what I'm talking about.

Not that I'm borrowing trouble, not anymore. I have finally sworn off my old habit of trying to prepare for life's losses and grief, for the simple reason that it doesn't work. Jake's death made it painfully clear: no amount of rehearsal reduces the sorrow of losing somebody you love. So you may as well love with an unfettered heart. If Eli can do it, I can, too.

Two other horses have moved here with us, first from Pegasus, then from Eva's barn. I derive a measure of security from their owners, Sandy and Robyn, a mother and daughter who've watched out for my horse for so long that I've come to regard them as godmothers of sorts. They have two horses. One, a massive draft, lives outside. The other is a cranky Quarter Horse that occupies the stall two doors down. Whenever we pass him, which is often, he never fails to pin his ears and bare his teeth at Eli.

That doesn't stop Eli from greeting his barnmate like a long-lost pal every time we walk by. Nor does Eli ever seem disappointed at not having his friendly overtures returned in kind. If anything, he seems reassured, his relative status confirmed. I can only guess that for a herd animal, being liked runs a distant second to knowing your place.

With an hour's drive each way, I maintain my early morning schedule rather than risk getting stuck in commuter traffic. As a result, it takes me a while to meet the other boarders. All are female, more than half are adults, and there isn't a single one I don't like.

Better still, for the first time in memory, Eli appears to have a best friend, another off-the-track Thoroughbred, a skittish young bay gelding named Rumor whose paddock runs alongside Eli's. I watch them romp together, running the fence line, bucking and squealing, and chewing on each other's headgear in the popular equine game known as halter tag.

This isn't the first time Eli has kicked up his heels with a horse in a neighboring paddock, but there seems to be more to this friendship than hijinks and horseplay. On the aisle, while I'm trying to groom him, Eli insists on keeping Rumor in his sights, a tricky thing because Rumor has a habit of dozing in the back of his stall. And more than once, when I've slogged through the mud to Eli's paddock, carrots in hand, to bring him in or to say good-bye, I've found him standing watch over his sleeping buddy, refusing to budge, not even for his favorite treats. Although inconvenient, I find his devotion heartwarming.

I'm happy for him, knowing how long and how hard he has searched for a pal, only to be rudely rebuffed. But I worry about what will happen if Rumor's owner decides to bring him home to her own three-stall barn, something she's seriously considering. She assures me that if she does, she'll bring another of her horses to take Rumor's place. But with horses, as with people, I'm not sure close friends are so easily replaced.

Once again, I find myself wrestling with my decision to turn Eli out by himself. It's been years since I've tried putting him in a paddock with another horse, unlike most of the horses that live here. The geldings, with a few exceptions, go out as a group in one of the bigger paddocks, as do the mares. Hard as it is to watch Eli get turned out alone, he's so guileless, so friendly, so utterly oblivious to pinned ears, bared teeth, and poised legs, I can only imagine what kind of shape he'd be in by the time he figured out what this posturing means.

In the end, I decide once again not to risk it, but rather to leave things as they are. It turns out to be the right choice because Rumor's owner takes him home, and though Eli undoubtedly misses him, their separation would've been far more traumatic had they shared a paddock as opposed to a fence line.

Now that we're settled in a place we both like, it's clearly time to start riding again. Instead, I keep manufacturing excuses, and I'm accomplished at that, at least.

Why am I dragging my feet? Out of fear? In ten years, I've come off Eli no more than a handful of times. In addition to the puddle incident at Oakwood, I've logged only three other spills, all of them at Pegasus. Once, when Mike's dog suddenly ran past the gate to the indoor just as we approached, Eli spun around and took off at a gallop. Despite having lost a stirrup in his initial 180, I stayed on for what seemed like an eternity before getting bounced off in a jarring downward transition.

My next fall occurred on a cold winter day when I'd underestimated Eli's energy by half. Again, he'd spun and bolted; all I remember about this particular unplanned dismount is him launching me into the middle of somebody else's lesson, embarrassing to say the least.

Even when you're lucky enough to avoid injury, falling from a horse, particularly a running one, is always a shock to your system. No sooner do you realize you're falling than the ground rushes up and clobbers you hard in the face. Often, upon landing, the first breaths you take deliver no oxygen at all, leaving you gasping for air and panicking over the fact that you're not getting any.

At that point, you may become aware of a little voice telling you to stay down; depending on whether you've been riding alone, it may be the voice of your trainer or that of the rational half of your brain. Either way, your next move might very well be determined by the whereabouts of your horse. Has Elvis left the building? Or is he still running around in the ring?

My most recent fall occurred during a lesson with Karen, as Eli and I were cantering toward a side wall. It was definitely pilot error: I failed to adequately commit to a direction in time for him to know which way to turn. As a result, he went right and I went left. I also fractured a rib, my first broken bone in all the years I'd been riding. I didn't even know it until days later, when I finally went to the doctor for painkillers. It turns out a broken rib hurts like hell.

Nonetheless, it didn't stop me from riding again as soon as I could get on without wincing. So what the hell is my problem this time?

Because I can still hear Jackie and Karen berating me in my head, I can only surmise that I've internalized their voices. Regardless of how many times I've tried telling myself I'm a competent and capable rider, years of insults have finally superseded my effort to keep a good thought. I have turned a deaf ear to my own attempts at empowerment. All I can hear is the shouting.

The resident trainer at our new barn, a cheerful and vibrant young woman named Christee, seems to have a large and loyal clientele, but I'm too wary of trainers to approach her. I've yet to find one who could teach without screaming. On the other hand, I clearly need help.

So I hover in the background and keep my ears open whenever I see Christee giving a lesson. I don't know what to make of a trainer who never raises her voice beyond what's necessary in order to be heard from the other end of the ring. I can only conclude she must not be very good.

That's bullshit, of course, and I know it. *I* am the one who is not very good. And as long as I stay off my horse's back, nobody has to find out.

Not that I'm happy not riding. In fact, I am miserable. I can barely look Eli in the eye. When I do, I see boredom and disgruntlement. God knows I have no trouble living with my own unhappiness, but I'm having a difficult time living with his.

And so, with Beth's encouragement, I finally approach Christee. Just to be on the safe side—and to gird myself from further disappointment—I make it a point to tick off all the reasons she probably won't want to work with us: a middle-aged woman with post-traumatic stress disorder from too many screaming trainers, and a middle-aged Thoroughbred with a bad right front wheel and an unfortunate tendency toward mishap and misfortune.

Christee says she'd be happy to.

So I trot out my ace in the hole: my ridiculous early morning schedule, which I can't imagine being workable for her.

She says no problem.

I mention how long it's been since I've ridden.

I throw in the fact that I had polio as a child.

"Are you done?" she asks, still smiling.

I ponder that for a moment. "I think so. Yes."

"Great! Let's get started."

So we do, and little by little I find myself trusting this unflappably sunny young woman who seems to like and respect not only Eli but me, who pushes us just enough and never yells, regardless of how much I test her.

"How come you haven't said anything about my position?" I ask, as Eli and I trot a big circle around her.

"I haven't said anything because your position is fine," she replies.

"What about my hands, then? My hands must be terrible."

"Your hands are fine, too."

"Liar."

Because she is so unassuming, Christee is forever impressing me with how much she knows, never more so than when I see her on her own horse, a very large, very overwrought train wreck of a horse, whose previous owner gave him to her for nothing.

Beautiful as he is, at 17.5 hands, Franz is one big, scary horse, and Christee makes no bones about the fact that he also scares her on a regular basis. But little by little, she's earning his trust in much the same way she's earned mine. And if I liked her before, I like her that much more now, for being not only a gutsy rider but an honest one.

I also like the way she rides Eli, and the way she brings out all the stuff that he knows. After years of listening to Karen complain about how difficult he was to ride, it's good to know someone else finds him fun. When I compliment her, Christee turns the tables on me. "You're the one who taught him all this," she says. Even though that may be a touch generous, it's also more or less true. And naturally, I never tire of hearing it.

She teaches me how to long-line him, a training technique that enables me to work Eli from the ground with no weight on his back, a technique that turns out to be nowhere near as dangerous or difficult as previous trainers had led me to believe.

Eli quickly gains strength and rebuilds muscle, and I begin to recoup some of the riding ability I'd thought lost. Mark, our talented farrier, recommends a hoof supplement that starts to make a difference sooner than I would have thought possible, and Eli seems more comfortable than he has in some time.

Back on the home front, try as I may, I can no longer handle the silence. I tell my husband it's time, that I've had my fill of life without a dog. I do some research that culminates in a Massachusetts-bred black Lab puppy, an adorable holy terror we name Huck. Not after Huckleberry Finn, as is widely assumed, but rather "my huckleberry friend" from "Moon River," which I sing to him on the long car ride home in a futile attempt to drown out his yowling: "Two drifters, off to see the world . . ."

Any secret notion I might have harbored about replacing my beloved Jake with a younger, bouncier version of him is put to rest the minute we get the new puppy home. Our house quickly fills up with his handiwork: shredded newspapers, torn-up foam rubber cushions, chewed chair rails.

Stubborn, demanding, affectionate, Huck is nothing like Jake. Nor is he any harder to love.

fifteen

LABOR DAY WEEKEND 2007

M Y BIRTHDAY, THE LAST DAY OF AUGUST, has always been a slightly mixed bag, mostly festive, but with a wisp of ennui. I wouldn't call it melancholia or regret, not exactly, just a tinge of a darker ethos that seeped in along with the ice cream and cake.

Looking back on it now, it seems painfully obvious why my eagerness was always tempered with dread: my birthday also marked the end of summer vacation, the last good thing before the new school year began. There may have been more to it, but as a Virgo, I'm prone to overanalyzing, so I think I'll just leave it at that.

In any event, on this, the day after my fifty-third birthday, I'm still preoccupied, still in post-birthday mode. I've just hopped on my horse and am warming him up on a loose rein in the indoor ring while Christee clears away jumps to give us more room to work.

I become aware of the voice in my head trying to get my attention, telling me to snap out of my reverie and get my wits about me, lest I end up on the ground. *Why,* I wonder. Then I feel the answer and *know* why: Eli is vibrating underneath me, the way he does just before he blows up.

I call over to Christee: "Eli feels a little high."

She straightens up from dismantling a jump and watches us for a minute. "He looks okay to me."

"Okay." I decide not to worry about it for once.

The first buck comes out of nowhere, pitching me forward onto his neck; the second—a real beauty, all four feet off the ground—launches me into the air. I'm just thinking how odd it feels to be suddenly soaring through nothingness like an ejected fighter pilot when I hit the dirt hard on my left side.

In the seconds it takes for my wind to return, I already know:

- That I will be able to breathe again shortly, as soon as the spasms in my diaphragm subside.
- That while I've undoubtedly done some damage, I had best take advantage of the adrenaline rush to grocery shop before the real pain kicks in, since my in-laws are coming for dinner and I have nothing whatsoever in the house.
- That I'll probably never know with any certainty whatever possessed my horse to buck me off for the first time in eleven years.

＊＊＊

DINNER BECOMES TAKEOUT PIZZA. Even though I'm still hours away from feeling the full effects of my fall, nobody wants me to cook.

I acquiesce, though I'm still standing fast on my refusal to go to the emergency room on a holiday weekend. I insist I can tough it out until Tuesday, should I decide I am going at all.

By Labor Day, however, Mark's had enough of watching me struggle to lie down and get up again. He takes me to the hospital, where a CT scan shows I've broken my eleventh and twelfth ribs, the so-called "floating" ribs. The ones that aren't attached at the front of the body. The ones that move every time the rib cage flexes, in other words, whenever you breathe, cough, sneeze, or laugh. In short, the ribs you do not want to break.

After a couple of shots of morphine, though, I'm considerably happier and more comfortable than I've been in three days. For a time, I'm on supplemental oxygen, too, and while I am, life is like a box of chocolates.

But then the ER doctor takes it away to monitor my oxygen levels with me breathing on my own. Apparently, they're nothing to write home about. He wants to admit me, to which I say "No way, José," two shots of morphine having turned me into a five-year-old.

In the end, he reluctantly agrees to send me home with an incentive spirometer, a charming device I'm supposed to breathe into slowly and deeply in a series of repetitions several times a day. The device has an indicator that will enable me to monitor my lung function; the deeper my breathing, the better. I also have to promise to see my own doctor right away.

It's late by the time we get home. I slowly and carefully lower myself into bed, inch by inch, to the point where I finally have to let go and free-fall the rest of the way. I then slip into a morphine-induced near coma for the better part of ten hours, my last good night's sleep for a very long time.

⋆

THE SIMPLE ACT OF DONNING MY JEANS has taken on a degree of difficulty normally reserved for Olympic gymnastics. Bending over to pull on my socks? Fuggedaboutit.

"You about ready?" Mark calls from downstairs, where he is waiting to take me to see my doctor.

"Gee, I don't know. Can I go topless?" I'm a little testy, as would anyone be who can no longer laugh without wanting to cry.

In the time it takes to dress my injured body, I have ample opportunity to recall various conversations over the years about knowing when to hang up your spurs. The first such discussion I remember being privy to took place in the tack room at Oakwood, where a bunch of us had been pissing and moaning about our sore this and aching that. We quieted down when Edith, white-haired and in her sixties, poked her head in to look for her gloves. The minute she'd gone, though, someone had asked, "How do you know when you're too old to ride?"

For a moment, nobody said anything. Then Jackie spoke up: "You just do."

At the time, I was only just starting to learn; the concept of being too old barely registered. That had been just over ten years ago. I'm still not too old. Nowhere near.

My doctor, a sweet, gentle man with a kind face and weary eyes, has known me a very long time. He isn't a big Eli fan, but I can't hold that against him. All he ever gets to see is the downside.

He listens to my heart and my breathing, reads the ER doctor's report, and writes me a prescription for Tylenol 3's. Getting in and out of the car is on a par with getting in and out of bed: excruciating. By the time I get home, I'm worn out. I briefly consider the bed before opting for the recliner.

Discomfort aside, I miss Eli. I've been getting updates on him from both Christee and Beth, so I know that he misses me, too. After a few days without seeing me, he invariably gets cranky. As do I after not seeing him.

Mark has offered to drive me to the barn for a visit, which I appreciate, but I want to go by myself. I miss the early morning commute: the "me" time that gives me a chance to reflect. And besides, with Mark along Eli won't be the same. He'll be distracted and I want him focused on me.

So after a short test drive to do a couple of errands, I feel physically ready to return. Not to ride, of course, just to visit. I pick up a big bag of carrots, get up early the next morning and go.

I'm a little nervous for some reason, which seems strange at first; but then again, maybe not. Although I'm reasonably certain Eli can't connect the dots linking his bucks to my fall, and my fall to my absence, his reaction to Missy weeks after he kicked her makes me wonder whether I'm underestimating him.

As I get closer, I start to feel butterflies in my stomach. What am I so worried about? That he'll feel guilty? That he'll turn away from me the way he turned away from Missy? Yup, I think that sounds about right.

By the time I leave the highway and head up the steep hill to the barn, all my nervousness fades. As I turn down the driveway and see Eli hanging his head out his window, I see only beauty.

He calls to me and I hear only music.

By October, when Mark and I head to Spain for a long-planned adventure, I've recovered sufficiently to hoof it all around Barcelona, San Sebastian, Bilbao, and Madrid, though it's a few more weeks before I can comfortably sleep on my left side.

By that time, I'm riding again.

* * *

FOR A MIDDLE-AGED WOMAN who's nowhere near ready to stop riding, there is no greater shot in the arm than Equine Affaire, an annual four-day extravaganza held in Columbus, Ohio, in the spring, and North Springfield, Massachusetts, in the fall.

"North America's Premiere Equine Expositions & Equestrian Gatherings" draw tens of thousands of horse owners and horse enthusiasts, 79 percent of them female. And 79 percent of *them* are over the age of thirty-five. Although I'd heard of Equine Affaire, what little I knew was mostly related to the emptiness of various barns over the years whenever the Massachusetts event was going on— that, and the bags and bags of merchandise that would accompany the other boarders upon their return.

In addition to the 230 clinics, seminars, and demonstrations on various equestrian sports and horse training methodologies presented by Olympians and world and national champions, Equine Affaire is the largest horse-related trade show in the East, with more than 400 retailers, manufacturers, service providers, and organizations. The vendors fill five exhibit halls with everything from saddles and riding apparel to horse trailers and artwork.

"You're kidding," Christee says, when I confess I've never been.

She immediately takes charge, deciding we should stay overnight in order to see Pfizer Fantasia, an evening equine musical revue choreographed to music of varying tempos, showcasing professional performers in disciplines ranging from driving to dressage and from reining to trick riding.

The first thing I notice as we stream through the gates in the sleet the morning of opening day is the size of the crowd; the next is the demographics. For the first time in my life, I'm surrounded by horse-loving women of a certain age. Most are decked out in all of their horse-loving glory, from the Western riders' hand-tooled cowboy boots, silver belt buckles, and fringed leather jackets to the dressage queens in their sleek quilted vests, formfitting jeans, and black boots. The ground is muddy, the atmosphere charged, the scene, like an equestrian Woodstock.

For the next two days, Christee and I race from clinic to seminar to demonstration, watching top riders and renowned trainers and learning right along with them. We visit the Breed Pavilion to get a firsthand look at types of horses neither of us has ever seen, and we check out the horse trailers, round pens, stalls, barns, and other heavy equipment we would buy if money were no object. And then we shop, loading up on free samples of feed, treats, and supplements as we go.

The checkout lines are long, but the easy camaraderie among those waiting helps the time pass. We meet horse-women from all over the world, comparing notes on everything from board fees to cribbing collars. We also run into old friends.

By the time we head home, I've seen enough to know I never want to miss Equine Affaire again, and I never do. Christee and I have been back every year.

sixteen

SPRING 2008

RAW, RAINY SUNDAY IN APRIL. Eli, running laps in the indoor ring, suddenly takes a bad step. Our eyes lock for an instant; I see pain, fear, confusion. He sees horror.

He can't stop right away; there's no jockey to pull him up, and he's moving too fast for me to grab. He'd been at it too long, a big chestnut blur galloping around and around at breathtaking speed. I should have stopped him. Why didn't I? I was chatting, not paying attention.

This is my fault.

I forget how to breathe as I watch him hobble another half lap around, doing God knows how much more damage before hitting the brakes, finally. We race over, my trainer and I. Christee feels his left front while I hold his head and try to soothe him. A thin sheen of sweat coats his neck, which feels slick and hot under my hand. He is trembling. It takes us fifteen minutes to get him out of there, one brutal step at a time, inching our way to the hose, baby steps, so we can run cold water over the leg before it swells.

I think of Barbaro. I think of Eight Belles, euthanized on the track minutes after her second-place finish in the 2008 Kentucky Derby, with fractures in her cannon and sesamoid bones. It's impossible not to think of them, along with all the other, less celebrated Thoroughbreds like mine, horses that shattered their bones as they ran, doomed by their own engineering.

The cold water doesn't help. We add insult to injury, squirting two grams of the bitter bute-paste painkiller down his throat. I fluff up his stall with an extra bag of pine shavings and throw in an armload of hay, things you do when your horse is hurt and you are helpless. I go stand by his head and feed him carrots—the first tastes like bute, so he spits it back out—then I talk to him softly, pianissimo, while he chews.

I tell him I'm sorry. I don't know yet what's wrong, but I can see he's in a great deal of pain. I ask him to stand quietly. I promise I'll get the vet here first thing in the morning, and we'll figure this out and we'll fix it. Hang in there, I tell him. I love you.

We are eyeball to eyeball, my racehorse and I, mine blue, his a rich caramel brown with gold flecks and a fringe of stiff reddish lashes that tickle my face as he blinks. I kiss the little dent over one worried eye, the furry spot beneath his ear, the perfect white star on his chestnut forehead.

I stay until long after the sweat has dried and his racing heart has slowed back down to its normal rate, sometimes talking, sometimes trying to slow my heart rate, too, remembering to breathe, telling myself not to panic. I remind him that we've been in tight corners before. "We'll get through this, too," I whisper. "Don't worry. We will."

When his head starts to droop, I tiptoe out of his stall and get in the car for the hour drive home. To walk the dog. To make Mark's dinner. To lie awake half the night. To flog myself for having let this happen. To make deals with God or the Devil until dawn, when it will finally be time to return.

✦ ✦

GOD HELP ME, SHE'S TOO YOUNG. The vet is too young, and she hasn't even brought the right stuff. There's no X-ray machine, no ultrasound. She feels Eli's left front leg, zeroing in on the shoulder, then watches him take a few agonizing steps. She winces. "Put him back in his stall."

Her name is Kim Harmon, and she's fresh out of vet school: Pennsylvania, so at least I know she's smart. I follow her out to her truck, where she loads me up with painkillers and writes out a schedule for their use. I'm to check in with her the following day. We make tentative plans for her to come back with the X-ray machine the day after that. In the meantime, Eli is not allowed out of his stall.

"Not even to clean it?"

"Clean around him," she says, and is gone.

The barn fee is $95—that's just for her to walk in the door, apart from medication or anything else she might do, and I've just spent it learning absolutely nothing. At the rate we're going, it will be days before I know the extent of the damage, before I know the prognosis, before I can sleep at night.

Back in the barn, I find Eli in the same position as when I left him, leaning against the back wall of his stall. It's a good stall, airy and bright and slightly bigger than the rest. I pay a little extra for it, but I'm happy to do that for him. It's worth it to see him hang his head out the window and watch for my car, to hear his throaty greeting in the mornings.

I grab a handful of carrots and am about to go in when I see his head drop. Nap time. I want to stay with him, even if all I can do is to just watch him sleep, but I know that the more rest he gets, the better. So I whisper "Sleep tight" and go home.

Day Three: I call Kim from the barn to report he's no better, and to ask a favor. "Please don't be offended. It's nothing personal, but if I'm going to be facing a horrible decision, I'm going to need someone with a bit more experience to advise me."

I hold my breath as I wait for her reply, which will be telling. What I'm hoping she'll say is that I'm being silly; that whatever he's done, it will not do him in.

Instead, she says: "I understand totally. I would never presume to tell you what to do. I'll bring someone more senior with me."

I think: if I cover the mouthpiece, maybe she won't hear me cry.

* * *

I KEEP CALLING CHRISTEE at her day job, pestering her with questions I know she can't answer: Why didn't we stop him? What do you think it is? Do you think it's broken or just bruised? Aren't there bones a horse can break and still recover?

"I don't know."

"I know you don't *know*, but what do you *think*?"

"I don't think it's broken," she says finally.

"Why not? Based on what?" (This is me hammering her for trying to be reassuring.)

"Gut feeling. I just don't think it is."

Neither does the senior vet who accompanies Kim the next day to take endless X-rays of Eli's left shoulder, pulling his leg straight out in front of him, then bending the knee, manipulating it in ways I imagine are causing him unspeakable pain that he's too groggy and doped up to protest.

From my own lengthy experience with bad ultra-sounds, I know better than to try to glean anything useful from a screen. Instead, I've learned to watch faces, which are far more revealing than some shadowy image, especially on the older machines. It doesn't take long for the person operating the probe to stop smiling when she sees something terribly wrong.

At the moment, the fact that both vets are displaying vertical frown lines between their eyebrows suggestive of deep concentration speaks to their uncertainty as to what they are seeing. I keep my eye on them, though, lest I see them relax their mouths or raise their eyebrows to indicate comprehension.

Under the influence of the fast-acting sedative, Eli's fine Thoroughbred head feels like an anvil in my arms. His droopy lips leak saliva all over the protective lead apron that covers my chest. "It's okay," I whisper into his lifeless right ear, slack as a donkey's. "They're almost done. It's okay."

The two vets huddle over their X-ray machine, trying to gauge whether they have their shot. Shoulders are hard to X-ray, they tell me. So much muscle mass. A few more, just to be on the safe side.

I shift my weight, propping Eli's head a little higher, feeling the ache in my back, welcoming it. So far, they're not seeing a fracture, but that doesn't mean it's not there. The surgeon will review the X-rays later. He's better at spotting these things.

I know what they're looking for: A stress fracture thin as a crack in a glass, somewhere along his left shoulder blade; a common racehorse injury caused by repetitive force, typically galloping. If caught in time, I'm pretty sure a stress fracture can heal, but it takes months and requires immobilization lest it propagate into the joint.

If Eli has a stress fracture that extends into a joint, I am going to lose him.

Kim grabs his tail to steady him as I help my poor drunken gelding back into his stall, taking out every last wisp of hay, anything he could choke on. He'll get it back when he's fully alert. I watch him sleep, wondering how many times I've done this very thing, waiting for a sedative to wear off, for him to open his eyes. Wanting to be the first person he sees when he's sick or scared, stressed or defenseless.

"He's such a nice horse," Kim says, watching me watch him, "And such a good patient."

"He's had plenty of practice," I reply, "unfortunately."

"How far do you want to take this?" she asks. "You need to be thinking about that."

I listen without comprehension, as if she's speaking a language I don't understand.

But I do, of course. That night I have the nightmare: I'm leading Eli to a giant hole in the ground. He goes trustingly, willingly, with no sense of betrayal, snatching the occasional mouthful of grass as we go, each step bringing him closer to the prick of the needle, the very last thing he will feel on this earth. I wake up in a panic.

Leading a horse to his own freshly dug grave is actually a best-case scenario. A horse that dies in a stall ends up being dragged behind a tractor; one sold for slaughter goes to a rendering plant, to be processed along with rancid meat and unwanted dogs and cats into soap and cosmetics, crayons, candy, and lard.

I've mostly kept a respectable distance between my conscious mind and the notion of Eli's demise, reminding myself that he's only six, ten, fifteen, eighteen years old. Like people, horses are living longer, for many of the same reasons: advancements in medicine, nutrition, and care. Horses can live well into their thirties. Eli and I should have many more good years together.

But with the possibility of a broken shoulder blade, the brutal logistics of equine mortality are suddenly staring me in the face. The hole in the ground is nothing compared with the one he's going to leave in my life, a hole so huge it took 1,254 pounds to fill.

* * *

WHAT LITTLE TIME I HAVE at home is mostly spent doing chores, walking Huck, and girding myself for the following day. Somehow, I fix dinner, pay bills, and wash clothes; I'm on autopilot much of the time.

I know Mark feels helpless, as do my parents, my sister, my in-laws, my friends, but there's really nothing anyone can do. We can only wait for the surgeon who's better at spotting these things to render his verdict.

Finally, that night, Kim calls with the news, which has elements of both worst- and best-case. Eli's shoulder blade is indeed broken, but the fracture doesn't extend into the joint, at least not yet.

Not yet? I struggle to process this, to follow what the young vet is saying and react to it more or less at the same time. Her words are simple enough, but ever since the phone rang, I've been in some kind of time warp. My ability to understand basic language and form reasonable conclusions seems to have slowed to a crawl.

She goes on. If all goes well, we are looking at a minimum of four months in his stall. That means he won't be allowed out until August at the soonest. It's overwhelming to think about—he'll miss the rest of the spring and most of the summer—but at least we have a fighting chance. This, at last, I'm able to grasp, and I'm grateful. I'm also touched by the relief immediately visible on Mark's face when I tell him the news could be worse.

When I lay out the situation for Beth the next morning, I remind her that the fracture could easily propagate if Eli isn't kept quiet; should that happen, it's all over for him. "So we're going to have to be supercareful, especially as he starts to feel better. Keeping him in his stall won't do any good if he bounces around in there, so we're going to have to do—"

"Whatever it takes," she finishes it for me.

At that, I'm finally able to stop my nervous nattering and take a deep breath, then another. As I do, my silence makes room for my first hopeful thought in the better part of a week: *This is why we're here. This is why Eli and I came to Dragonfly. We're in the right place to get through this.*

I rearrange my schedule, crowding out all nonessential activities—everything, pretty much—so that I can spend time with Eli six mornings a week. For the first month or so, I'm not quite as terrified at the prospect of him doing more damage, because he's in too much pain to want to move around much. Just in case, though, I stock up on acepromazine, called "ace" around barns, the injectable sedative most often given to quell anxiety in horses. As Beth says, *whatever it takes.*

I also cut way back on his grain, one of the first things I know to do in situations like this, because there's little point stoking a fire that should not—that cannot—be lit. Eli won't be burning anywhere near as many calories as he normally would, so he won't need anywhere near as much fuel.

At the same time, we increase his hay ration to ward off hunger and help keep him occupied, thereby reducing some of the stress that tends to go along with being confined to a stall.

Now that the weather's getting better and more of the horses are living outside, as opposed to going out during the day and coming back inside at night, Beth arranges to bring another boarder's horse back in at midday to keep Eli company for a couple of hours. We hope that will relieve some of the isolation that comes with being the only horse in his barn.

My new morning routine consists of driving to Dragonfly before dawn, feeding Eli his tiny portion of breakfast grain, giving him a good grooming—as good as I can manage with him in his stall—and just hanging out with him for a while, feeding him carrots and shooting the breeze.

I then grab a big bucket or two and go scavenging for grass, the sweetest and best I can find. My mission usually takes me out behind the indoor or alongside the road in front of the house, areas where the horses aren't allowed to graze. I pull it up by the handful, hoping I've learned enough from years of grazing Eli to choose only the freshest blades, while he hangs his head out his window and anxiously awaits my return.

When I finally do reappear, the flare of his nostrils and the shrill vibrato of his welcoming whinny make it clear that second only perhaps to my initial approach with his carrots, this is the highlight of his day. If only grass didn't take quite so long for me to gather, or quite so little time for him to eat, I'd happily spend half the day filling buckets for him to snack on.

Instead, after two or three rounds, I leave a stash of carrots near his door for Beth and the other boarders to dole out to help break up his day after I'm gone. If seeing me coming is the best part of his day, driving away from him is the worst part of mine. It's then that my worrying reaches its zenith. Although I know I've done everything I can do for him that day, I still have an ache in my chest when I leave. The minute I can no longer see him, my mind's free to wonder whether I'll see him again.

And so it goes, six days a week for the first thirty days, a very long month during which nothing changes but the weather, increasingly sunny and warm, making it that much more difficult to see Eli cooped up in a stall, even a nice roomy one.

Our first milestone takes the form of a follow-up appointment with Kim, who comes to see how her patient is holding up. She gingerly moves him around in his stall, feels his shoulder and scratches his neck. Eli, in turn, rests his chin on her head, rearranges her dark hair into a style she's never considered, and blows on her neck. All in all, a good visit. We are all three of us pleased.

I walk her out to her truck. "Next time," she says, "I'll take some more X-rays to see how the bone is remodeling. In the meantime, keep up the good work."

"One down, three to go," I tell Eli after she leaves. "At this rate, you'll be back out in your paddock before you know it."

Three months actually seems like an eternity to me, but I'll be damned if I'll say that to him.

⋆_⋆⋆

AS WORD OF ELI'S INJURY SPREADS, so do the ranks of his visitors and supporters. It's the rare human who doesn't take a minute to pay his or her respects to the sociable chestnut gelding laid up in the corner stall.

The guys from the property maintenance company that stores its equipment on the premises make a point of lingering by Eli's open window on their way to the out-house, as do the employees of the septic service that comes periodically to pump out the tank. Meanwhile, a new horse arrives in the stall across the aisle, and I walk in one morning to find the owner's mom enjoying a cuddle with mine. "We just love Eli," she says. "We always feed him his treats."

Although I'm thankful to everyone who helps brighten his days, I make sure that the sign Beth has taped to his door remains prominently in place, the one that emphatically states that Eli is not to come out. One small mistake could be all that it takes to undo whatever good has been done.

As spring settles over the farm and the last gasp of winter gives way to soft breezes and cabbage-sized rhododendrons, it gets harder to turn away and head home after my visits. On the nicest days, when the early morning fog that shrouds the hilltop burns off to reveal fat bumblebees and emerald green grass, it becomes downright painful to leave.

When I'm not at the barn, scratching Eli's itchy spots and foraging grass by the bucketful, I think of him in the same small square footage day after day, week after week. I picture the other horses being led out into the sunshine, leaving Eli alone in the dimly lit barn. Regardless of what time it is when I think of him—in the middle of a sandwich or the middle of the night—I know he's still standing there, right where I left him.

Luckily, to be sure, he is tolerating his confinement better than I am, as I imagine myself locked in my bathroom for 120 straight days and wonder if I'm being fair asking the same thing of him.

The fact that it's spring and not fall—that it's *summer* he's going to be missing—only adds insult to his injury. Bad enough he should suffer a painful, slow-healing fracture; why couldn't this be happening in January instead of May? Many days, I find myself praying for rain.

I also wonder whether he understands on any level why he's not being allowed to go out, whether he knows he has a life-threatening injury. I add it to the list of questions I'm saving for Kim, who'll be back for another round of X-rays in a few days.

So far, we haven't had to resort to the tranquilizer, but I have no doubt the day is coming. Already, Eli's a bit more rambunctious than I'd like, though truth be told I'd prefer that he not move at all, that he stand there as though he were stuffed.

I wonder what Eli's upcoming X-rays will show, even as I worry about the ramifications of four months of standing idle. I know from my research that healthy bones grow as a result of the stress that's placed on them; to be rebuilt with greater strength, they must first break down. This rebuilding is known as remodeling, a normal physiological process that is ongoing throughout life. Where it goes awry, as in Eli's case, is when the rate of damage exceeds the rate of repair. There's obviously a fine line between the two.

Extended layups like the ones Eli has had to endure are among the risk factors for stress fractures, as are the longer periods of lower-intensity exercise that tend to follow them. Shorter bursts of *higher*-intensity exercise, on the other hand, can help prevent them.

The primary danger associated with a stress fracture— that it will progress into a complete fracture—lessens over time. But here again, there's a fine line between a slowly strengthening bone and an idle horse that's about had it with doing nothing.

For the most part, though, I can't complain about Eli's attitude throughout his ordeal. Ironically, I credit his previous layups for giving him the inner resources to tolerate this one. If there's one thing my horse has learned, it's how to be a good patient. As long as he's getting his fair share of attention—and more than his fair share of carrots— he's proving himself remarkably self-possessed. It turns out the women from our first barn were right: for a Thoroughbred, he *is* much more sensible than most.

₊

THE NEW X-RAYS REVEAL what Kim believes to be active remodeling of Eli's shoulder blade along the fracture, though the subtlety of the images makes it difficult to say for sure. But the fact that he's moving a bit easier—judging from the tiny bit of movement he's allowed—seems to buttress her theory. I'm more than happy to have some encouraging news.

Now halfway through his four-month stall sentence, Eli has developed a new routine, one I've pieced together with Beth's help. After I leave, she says, he eats his morning hay and takes his nap. When he's through napping, he goes to work on his lunch hay. Next, he hits her up for a carrot or two when she comes back to muck out his stall. He then cribs on his window sill and hangs his head out to watch the others till dinner is served.

I am touched by his resilience, and by his ability to deal with his vastly shrunken life by breaking it into little chunks of activity, however modest. I've always felt he had a very good mind for a horse, but having put him to the ultimate test, I now know it for sure.

* * *

STALL-BOUND OR NOT, Eli's feet are continuing to grow, though not as quickly as they would if he were working. Although we've put it off for as long as possible, there comes a point at which he definitely needs a trim. Our farrier, Mark, has been kept in the loop with regard to Eli's shoulder injury. Unfortunately, I have a doctor's appointment I'm unable to change on the day Mark will trim Eli's feet, but I'm not worried about not being there.

As he'll want to see Eli take at least a few steps both in his old and new shoes, I arrange for Beth to stand in for me. I ask her to call me as soon as they're done, just so I know all is well.

I return from my appointment to a message on my machine and I immediately hit play, eager to hear how it went. I'm listening to Beth's message—that Eli's been shod, that everything's fine, that she walked him for the farrier before and after. Then I hear her say something that about stops my heart: "So then I took him outside and let him eat grass for a while. I hope that's okay."

No. She couldn't possibly have said that. I must've heard wrong. Poor reception, no doubt. I replay the message. There's no mistaking it this time.

How the hell is Eli supposed to know why it was okay for him to go out and eat grass today but not tomorrow? I can only imagine what's coming, the fury I'll face. And who could blame him?

I pick up the phone and punch in Beth's number, furiously stabbing the keypad with my finger, pushing the wrong buttons once, twice, three times. I finally get her machine, and it's all I can do to contain myself as I wait for the beep: "No, IT IS *NOT* OKAY TO TAKE ELI OUT TO EAT GRASS, AND YOU KNOW THAT. WHAT THE *HELL* WERE YOU THINKING?"

I then hang up and lose it completely.

I've calmed down considerably by the time she calls back. Even though I appreciate her apology, I get the distinct impression she thinks I'm overreacting by a power of ten. Rather than get into it over the phone, I hang up as soon as I can.

That night, unable to sleep, I lie awake and count my mistakes, all the bad choices I've made since buying Eli, beginning with chasing him around the indoor with a lunge whip at Oakwood and ending with not being with him to-day while the farrier trimmed his feet. *For want of a nail* . . .

The next morning, I'm filled with dread as I drag myself out of bed to go deal with Eli. I drive to the barn, feed him his breakfast, and give him as good a grooming as he's will-ing to stand still for. I then slip out of his stall and close the door behind me. That's when he erupts, right on cue.

He's on his hind legs, bouncing around in a fury; watch-ing him, watching the force with which he comes down on his fractured shoulder, I come unhinged. "STOP IT! JUST STOP IT! YOU WANT TO HURT YOURSELF WORSE?" Yelling at him is hardly the answer, but I can't help it. I'm every bit as out of control as he is.

Then Beth appears at my elbow. "I'm really sorry," she says, and this time there's no mistaking her remorse. "I didn't get what you were so upset about till after I'd talked to you."

"Look at him," I reply. "Now I *have* to drug him."

Yelling at Beth is as pointless as yelling at Eli. Besides, I can see she feels terrible. So I shut up and go into the tack room to fetch a syringe and my bottle of ace.

※

IN MANY WAYS, Eli's last month of confinement is the toughest. He's reaching his breaking point in terms of being cooped up in his stall. He's also feeling better. Given his track record with eleventh-hour shenanigans, I keep the ace handy and have no qualms about using it whenever I don't like the look in his eye.

I have to say, though, to his everlasting credit, Eli's al-ways been good about warning me when he's teetering on the brink of a meltdown. Even on the summer day when

I broke my ribs. Although I hadn't anticipated him bucking me off, I knew something was up. Had I acted on what I felt as opposed to what Christee saw, I could have avoided the entire episode.

Coulda, woulda, shoulda. I think I'll just file it under lessons learned. But as long as I'm on the subject, I've come to realize that for all I've learned from having owned my own horse, Eli has been trying to teach me the same lesson again and again for twelve years: trust yourself.

Thanks in large part to him, I finally do. Because there's really nothing the matter with me *or* my instincts, provided I listen to them. I know this because despite lethal parasites, deadly viruses, broken bones, and things that go bump in the night, Eli's still here.

And so am I.

* * *

KIM IS HALF AN HOUR LATE and I'm nervous. I keep glancing down at my watch, to the point where Eli has stopped eating the hay in his stall in favor of watching me watch the clock.

"Don't worry," I tell him for the umpteenth time, sliding yet another carrot out of the bag and dropping it into his feed bucket. "I'm sure she'll be here any minute."

He chews his treat slowly and thoughtfully, as if considering my words, then pokes his nose over his door to request another. Just to occupy myself, I decide to calculate the number of pounds of carrots I've fed him over the years. At a rate of about twenty pounds a week times fifty-two weeks a year times eleven and a half years—

Wait, on second thought, I have a better idea. Instead of carrots, I decide to count days, the number of days I've had Eli.

I fish a dull pencil out of the moldering collection next to the barn phone and tear a scrap of paper from a dusty notebook bearing the name of a boarder long gone. Eleven and a half years times 365 days . . . I do the math and come up with the answer: 4,197 days.

Small wonder I find it hard to remember my life before Eli. I do remember it, though. I remember it well enough to feel grateful, well enough to know I have him to thank for pulling me out of my dark, silent house. Now it's my turn. The symmetry pleases me.

I hear the crunch of tires on gravel and feel the fluttery sensation in my stomach that can only mean the vet is finally here. After all this time, I can hardly stand to wait for her to get off her cell phone and out of her truck. It's a beautiful day and I want Eli out in it immediately if not sooner.

I open his door and clip on a lead rope. Before I can walk him out onto the aisle, though, he reaches his head down to brush my cheek with his lips and rest his chin on my shoulder. I have no trouble translating these small, perfect gestures, both of them classic Eli: *Thanks, Mom.* We snuggle a moment, waiting to hear the truck door finally open and close.

"Am I interrupting something? Would you like me to come back another time?" I turn to find Kim standing there watching us, a big grin on her freckled face.

"Not on your life," I reply. I carefully lead Eli out of his stall and have him halt on the aisle so Kim can feel his shoulder. He stands perfectly still without flinching as she presses on it.

"Feels good," she says. "Why don't you walk him down and back?"

I turn him around in his stall, then walk him down the aisle to the other end of the barn, around the pole and back to where Kim is standing. "Great," she says, patting his neck. "You've done an amazing job."

"I've had help," I reply. Which reminds me: I poke my head out and catch a glimpse of Beth in the lower barn, having just finished turning out horses, and I holler to her to come quick. This is her moment, too, after all.

"Ready?" Kim asks.

I take a deep breath and nod. "Ready." Then, with the two of them looking on, for the first time in seventeen weeks, I lead Eli out of the dim barn and into the bright light of day.

Out of the stillness. Back into life.

CODA

With years a richer life begins,
The spirit mellows:
Ripe age gives tone to violins,
Wine and good fellows.
—JOHN TOWNSEND BROWBRIDGE

Please come help us celebrate
Eli's 20th birthday
Sunday, April 17th, 2010, 2 P.M.
Dragonfly Farm

In which we celebrate a milestone few thought we'd see
with a party in our barn and the guest of honor looking on
with a braided mane and a mouth full of carrot cake.

ACKNOWLEDGMENTS

MY GRATITUDE GOES FIRST AND FOREMOST TO MY AGENT, Susanna Einstein, who's kept my train on the tracks all these years with her incomparable blend of encouragement, wise counsel, and tough love. My heartfelt thanks to Renée Sedliar for being the kind of editor writers dream about, and to everyone at Da Capo Press for falling for Eli in the first place. Many thanks to Michele Wynn for careful copyediting and unbridled enthusiasm.

My deepest appreciation to Vicki and Erik Souza, brilliant wedding photographers who put gentility and romance aside and braved heat, bugs, and mud to come photograph Eli not once but twice, and to Alex Camlin, creative director extraordinaire, who turned one of those photos into a cover that captures Eli to a T.

I'm indebted to my husband, Mark Berns, for helping me let go of one dream in order to realize another, and for the myriad sacrifices he's made on my and Eli's behalf. I am beholden to my sister, Debbie Shulins, for sharing her children and for being there for me, distant in geography alone. Thanks to my parents, Arnold and Thelma Shulins, for their encouragement and support not only during the writing of this book but always.

I am grateful to my friend Thom Jones for urging me to write an animal book, and to my pal Claire Schoen for sharing her house so that I could write it without the distraction of unfinished chores. Thanks to my mother-in-law, Phyllis Curcio, and my friends John and Katie Gausepohl, Patti Reid, and Celia Maddox for reading early drafts and offering invaluable feedback.

My unending appreciation to past and present members of Team Eli, especially Drs. Robert Neff, Kim Harmon, and Rosemary Ganser, as well as Mark Reilly, Maggie Buck, Erik Heggland, and Dan Reilly. Without you—your dedication, expertise, and advice—this could have been a very short story.

And finally, I wish to express my admiration for the countless women who have cobbled together their families from hooves and hearts, feathers, and fur. You are all mothers in my book.